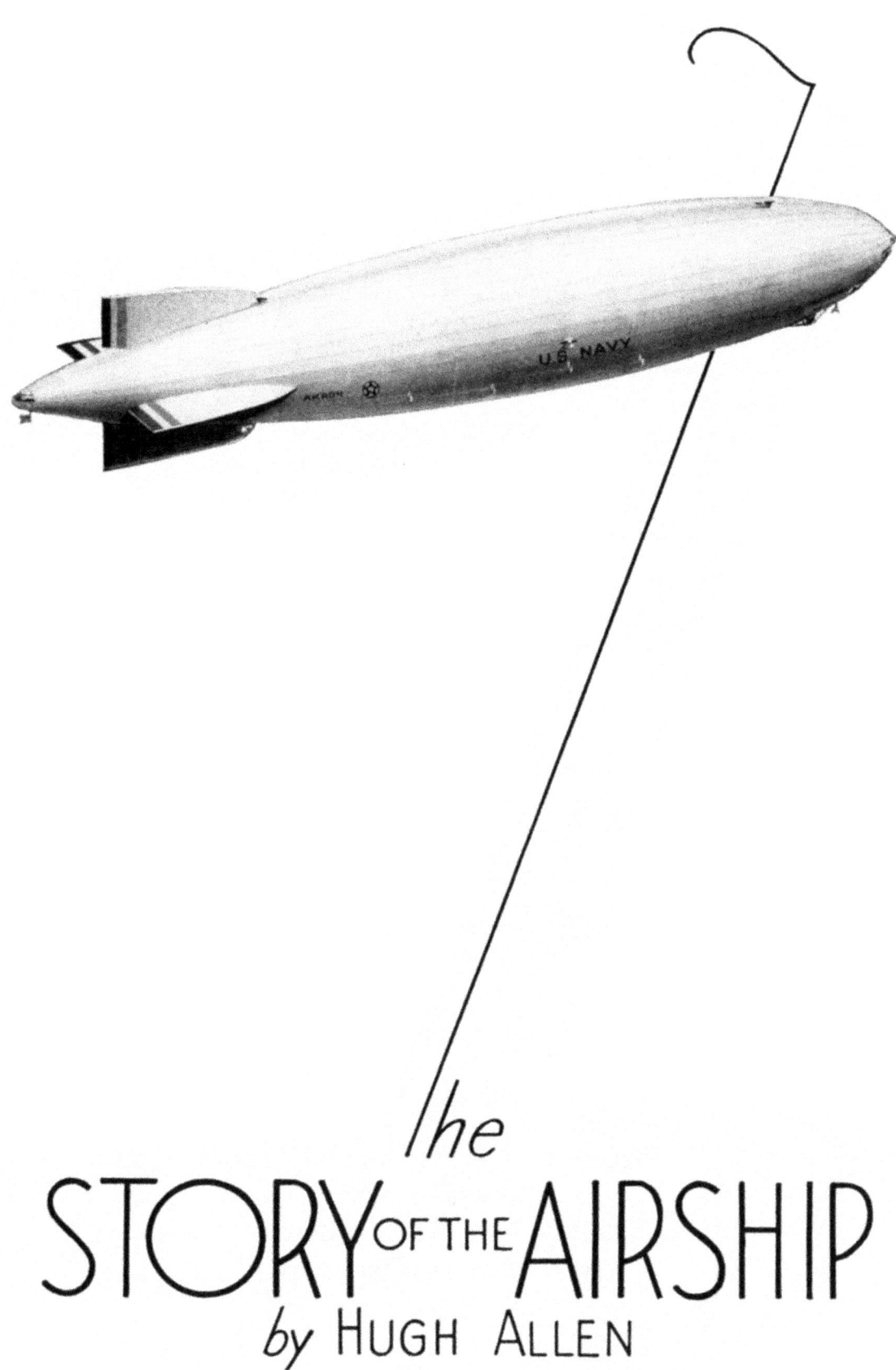

The STORY OF THE AIRSHIP
by Hugh Allen

Published annually since 1925 as a convenient
reference book for students, writers
and others interested.

Seventh Edition
Copyright, 1931
By The Goodyear Tire & Rubber Co.

This text has been digitally watermarked to prevent illegal duplication.

©2008-2010 PERISCOPE FILM LLC
ALL RIGHTS RESERVED
ISBN # 978-1-935700-04-3
WWW.PERISCOPEFILM.COM

Table of Contents

	PAGE
FOREWORD	1
CHAPTER	
I—The Airship and the Airplane	3
II—The Beginnings of Flight	5
III—Classes of Airships	8
IV—The Story of the Zeppelins	11
V—Goodyear in Aeronautics	15
VI—The Free Balloon	17
VII—Blimps or Air Yachts	19
VIII—Planning for the Naval Ships	24
IX—Building the Airship Dock	26
X—Improvements in Airship Design	32
XI—The New Navy Airships	34
XII—How the Akron Was Built	39
XIII—Safety of Rigid Airships	45
XIV—Helium and Duralumin	49
XV—Military Uses of the Airship	51
XVI—Airship Handling	55
XVII—Training Operations	60
XVIII—Commercial Air Liners	63
XIX—Notable Airship Flights	67
XX—Akron and Its Airport	68
AFTER WORD	71
APPENDIX	75
BIBLIOGRAPHY	83

THE STORY of the AIRSHIP

FOREWORD

By P. W. LITCHFIELD
President, The Goodyear Tire & Rubber Co. and
The Goodyear-Zeppelin Corporation

AERONAUTICS is transportation—whether of fighting men and materials of war, or of goods and peoples on peaceful missions—and civilization will find certain use for whatever craft can carry men and goods faster and farther than existing agencies.

The airplane and the airship can cover distances faster than any other vehicle devised by man. Men have ever been willing to pay a premium for speed, not for the sake of speed alone but because time and the saving of time has dollars-and-cents value.

The coincidence of superior transportation and national progress has happened too often in the history of nations to be dismissed as merely coincidence.

America, of all nations, needs no reminder of the value of transport, whether from an economic standpoint or the standpoint of national interest.

Transportation has been a potent factor in making the growth of the United States one of the amazing phenomena of industrial history. And, by the same token —and even more important—it has contributed tremendously to the result that from the Atlantic to the Pacific and from the Lakes to the Gulf, our people speak the same language, serve the same flag, respond to the same impulses and are guided by common ideals.

The airplane and the airship have shown merely a hint of new possibilities. How quickly those possibilities may become actualities in the economic life of the nation depends much less on mechanical improvements than on the realization by our people of those potentialities and their determination to explore and to capitalize them.

Better ships, better methods—these are but matters of engineering, of improved materials and machines, of the directing of the genius of the country to this problem.

* * *

THE airplane and the airship, sister craft, each supplementing and complementing the other, have each an important place in the commerce of the future.

The airplane is a somewhat more familiar figure to the general public than is the airship. There is still something of mystery to most people about these great silver cruisers of the air. And so this is primarily the story of the airship—designed to give, in simple words and briefly, the story of its history, its development, its potentialities for the future.

If America is to make wiser use of aeronautics than other nations its faith must be founded on facts, and its determination based on understanding.

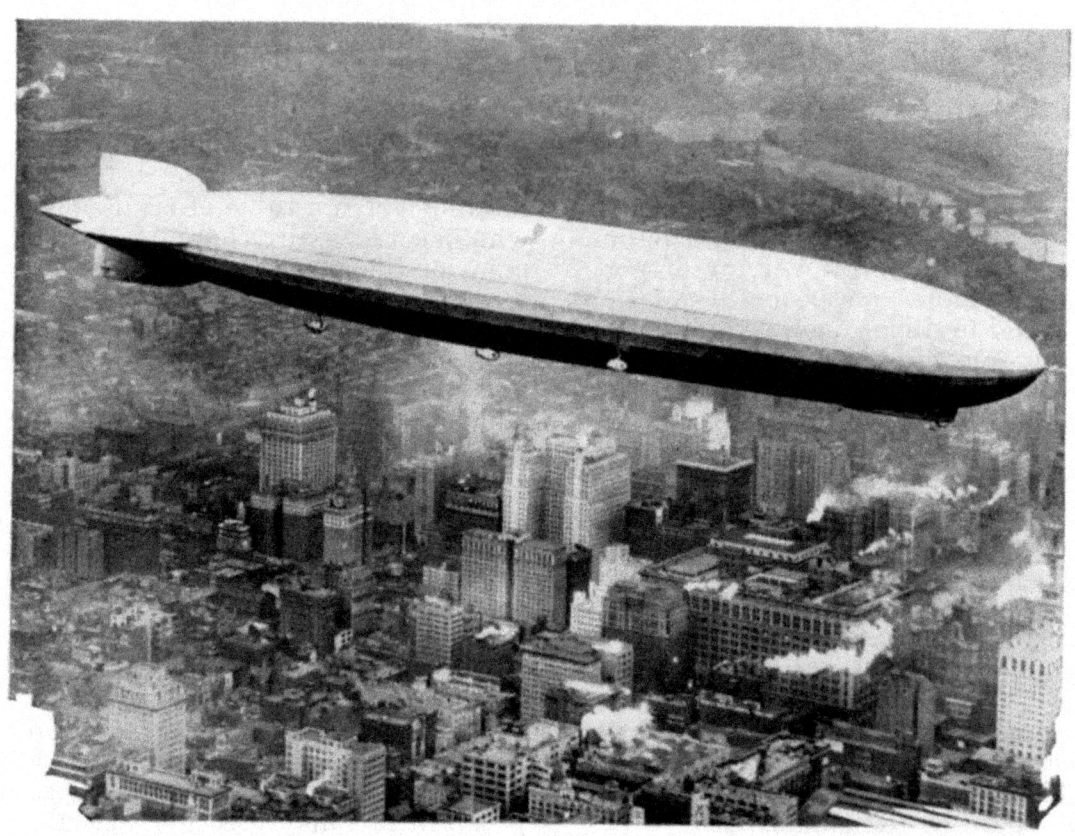

Graf Zeppelin in flight over Philadelphia. (Wide World Photo)

At the Los Angeles airport, the Graf Zeppelin and alongside it the airship Volunteer, stationed at Los Angeles.

CHAPTER I

The Airship and The Airplane

THIS is the story of the lighter-than-air ship. So perhaps one should start by making clear how it differs from the heavier-than-air plane.

They differ, first, in source of lifting power.

The airplane is a dynamic craft, deriving its lifting power from its velocity alone. The air pressure and suction on its wings give aerodynamic lift only as long as flying speed is maintained.

The airship is primarily aerostatic, that is its buoyancy arises from the fact that the lifting gas it contains is so much lighter than air that it will support, without other assistance, not only the balloon-like cells in which the gas is contained but the metal frame of the ship itself and the weight of crew, motors, fuel, and a pay load.

The airship continues to remain aloft even though its motors are shut off.

The airship, however, has an additional buoyancy, an aerodynamic lift resultant from motors and control surfaces.

The airship and the airplane differ again in that the airplane is primarily a fast comparatively short distance craft, while the airship is slower and comes into its full efficiency only on long voyages, particularly across oceans.

The cruising speed of most transport or mail planes carrying a pay load is 100 to 120 miles an hour with a radius of about 500 miles. Though naturally a specially built or special purpose plane can fly faster and further if pay load is replaced by fuel.

The airship, having a speed of 80 miles an hour and carrying ten tons of useful load, has been flown more than 6,000 miles in 69 hours with a comfortable fuel reserve at the end of the journey.*

While the transatlantic flights of the R-34, the Los Angeles, the Graf Zeppelin and the R-100 have indicated transoceanic flying as a logical field for the airship, there will still be controversy as to whether the airplane may not successfully challenge the airship here.

*See paper by Dr. Karl Arnstein, "Developments in Lighter-Than-Air Craft," given before Society of Automotive Engineers at Chicago, 1928.

Goodyear-Airwheel-equipped Fokker plane used for test purposes.

In discussing the subject before a meeting of the Society of Automotive Engineers in New York in May, 1930, former Commander J. C. Hunsaker, U. S. N., who had charge for the Navy of the design both of heavier-than-air craft and lighter-than-air craft during the war, stated his belief that:

"All successful Atlantic airplane flights may fairly be discounted as having been made by overloaded planes, without pay load, by abnormally courageous pilots, and in the most favorable summer weather that could be found. The unsuccessful airplane flights give mute testimony that good luck cannot be depended on.

"We do know, however," he continued, "that the modern airplane can fly the Atlantic provided one of several things does not happen. The things that must not happen are: first, persistent head winds causing exhaustion of fuel supply at sea; second, engine failure from any cause; third, loss of visibility with consequent loss of control and course and fourth, failure of any structural part or function of lifting, stabilizing or control surfaces.

"Each of these contingencies may be fatal to the airplane, and in this I include the flying boat or seaplane in the North Atlantic, as its chance of survival there on the surface of the sea is at best precarious. In low latitudes both in the Pacific and Atlantic, a flying boat has a very fair chance to remain afloat, but due to the infrequency of passing steamers many days may elapse before rescue. In general, a forced landing on the high seas cannot be tolerated by a commercial enterprise.

"The chance of a forced landing at sea due to exhaustion of fuel is measured by the margin of fuel carried versus the weather to be expected. We know that even with an overloaded start and no pay load and with favorable weather there has been practically no margin for those airplanes that have successfully negotiated the eastward crossing of the North Atlantic.

"We are building larger airplanes but their endurance unfortunately is not increasing. I need not here go into the aerodynamic and structural design principles which indicate only too clearly that mere increase in size gives no practical increase in en-

Fleet of six airships flying over the Goodyear-Zeppelin Corporation airdock where the U. S. S. Akron is being built for the Navy.

durance. There are gains in aerodynamic and structural efficiency due to changes in design made possible by very large airplanes, yet the effect of such gains is largely absorbed in overcoming the relative weight increase due to size itself."

CHAPTER II

The Beginnings of Flight

Count Ferdinand Zeppelin, founder of the German Zeppelin company in whose memory the Graf Zeppelin was named.

SINCE the beginnings of recorded time man has envied the bird its flight across the sky, above him. Now and then other men have watched smoke ascend to the clouds and travel on the winds, and some of them have visioned it a potential lifting force, and one that challenged human ingenuity.

It is not generally known, however, that the first passenger-carrying flight was made in 1783, more than a century before the Wright brothers—or that flying really began with lighter-than-air craft.

For in that year the brothers Montgolfier, Frenchmen, built a 35-foot paper balloon, suspended a brazier of charcoal below it and sent it aloft from the little French village of Annonay.

The Academy of Science, learning of the feat, summoned the Montgolfiers to repeat the demonstration in the capital.

But while the brothers were fashioning their second balloon, a Paris physicist named Charles constructed a silk balloon of approximately 1,400 cubic feet capacity, and, in August, 1783, sent it skyward inflated with hydrogen gas.

A month later, when the elder Montgolfier arrived in Paris and learned of the ascension of the Charles balloon, he decided to surpass his competitor by placing a sheep, a rooster and a duck as passengers aboard his balloon. This flight from the courtyard at Versailles was successful, the unusual cargo landing safely.

Today on the insignia of lighter-than-air officers of the U. S. Army Air Corps you may find tiny representations of a sheep, a rooster and a duck, reminiscent of Montgolfier's enterprise.

After this a young gallant of that day, named De Rozier, decided to be the first man in the world to make a free balloon flight, and in spite of the opposition of King Louis XVI, he sailed over Paris in November, 1783, in a balloon of Montgolfier construction while hundreds of Parisians applauded.

Benjamin Franklin was one of the witnesses of these earliest flights, and wrote home to friends in America:

Early type German Zeppelin airship resting on the water near its floating hangar.

5

"Among the pleasantries that conversation produces on this subject, some suppose flying to be now invented, and that since men may be supported in the air, nothing is wanted but some light handy instrument to give and direct motion. Some think progressive motion on the earth may be advanced by it, and that a running footman or a horse slung and suspended under such a globe so as to have no more of weight pressing the earth with their feet than perhaps eight or ten pounds, might with a fair wind run in a straight line across countries as fast as that wind, and over hedges, ditches and even waters. It has been even fancied that in time people will keep such globes anchored in the air, to which by pulleys they may draw up game to be preserved in the cool and water to be frozen when ice is wanted. And that to get money, it will be contrived to give people an extensive view of the country, by running them up in an elbow chair a mile high for a guinea."

Two years later, Blanchard, a Frenchman, and Dr. Jeffries, an American physician practicing in England, made the first balloon flight over the English Channel, leaving Dover at one o'clock in the afternoon and landing safely in Calais three hours later.

Balloons were used for military observation purposes during the French Revolution, in the American Civil War, and the Franco-Prussian War, and were utilized on a large scale in the World War.

The story of Gambetta's escape from Paris in 1870 when the city was surrounded by the Germans, an escape that undoubtedly prolonged the Franco-Prussian war, is well known. It is not generally realized however, that the French sent up 64 balloons during the last three months of the siege, carrying people and dispatches beyond the enemy lines. Two of these were blown out to sea and never heard from. The rest landed safely, including the "Ville d'Orleans" which caught a southwest wind and was carried across Germany and the North Sea, landing near Oslo, Norway, 15 hours later.

The essentials of free ballooning, including the gas-tight bag, the valve, the net, and the basket which carried the pilots, were all developed in the 18th century.

However, a balloon rides with the wind, and has no power to direct its course. So men looked about for methods of propelling them through the air. Though real success in this field was to wait for a dependable high-powered, lightweight engine, a score and more inventors whose names are long since forgotten worked for a century to verify Franklin's prophecy.

In 1852 Henri Giffard, a French inventor, built the first power-driven balloon, a dirigible, 145 feet in length deriving its motive power from a three-horsepower steam engine. Under favorable conditions this airship had a maximum speed of five miles an hour.

Through the half century following Renard, Lebaudy, Krebs, Haenlein, Tissenden, Juillot, Parseval, Knabenshue, Vaniman and many others experimented with more or less success, contributing to progress. Most spectacular, during this period, were the achievements of Santos-Dumont, a Brazilian residing in Paris who between 1906 and 1910 built 14 airships, with one of them taking a 100,000-franc prize for flying around the Eiffel Tower.

An Austrian named Schwartz constructed a rigid airship in 1898, using a framework and outer covering of aluminum, but it was destroyed on its first landing.

America's first military airship, a non-rigid type of 20,000 cubic feet capacity, was built in 1908 by the late Major Thomas S. Baldwin for the Army Signal Corps.

At the turn of the century, however, the long dreams of Count

1. Typical early German Zeppelin in flight. 2. Rear view of first Wright airplane. 3. Left in this picture are two early type ships built for army training work. Right are two free balloons. Upper left: Free balloon in flight at a National balloon race.

Zeppelin had begun to take form, for in 1900 he completed and flew his first craft and so laid the foundations of practicable commercial and military operations—a story, however, which will be related in a separate chapter.

The British, more conservative at the outset, became interested in rigid airships about 1910, built a small one, the Mayfly, and after 1914 became highly active in building non-rigid ships.

The American airship industry started also about 1911, when the government became interested, and at Akron The Goodyear Tire & Rubber Co. secured specialized machinery and initiated a scientific study of the subject.

From this small beginning came the establishment of great military bases and ships, while the year 1931 found Akron with a 1,000-acre airport within the city limits; a dock larger than any in the world; an assembly of technical experts and engineers building the world's greatest airship under plans that represented the accumulated experience of Germany and the United States in airship construction.

CHAPTER III

Classes of Airships

LIGHTER-THAN-AIR ships are divided into three classes: rigid, semi-rigid, and non-rigid. The essential structural difference is indicated by the names.*

The non-rigid is primarily a balloon, shaped to give directability, and carrying motors to give it forward movement. It maintains its shape by means of the pressure of the gas it contains. The popular name, blimps, indeed is derived from B-limp type, the British designation during the war to distinguish "limp" ships from rigid. An interesting feature of the non-rigid airships is an air-filled ballonet, built inside the cigar-shaped balloon with the result that, as the lifting gas expands, due to temperature or altitude, it forces air out of the ballonet, the gas supply being conserved. Conversely as the gas contracts more air is forced in from the slip stream of the propeller or by a blower.

The rigid airship has a complete metal structure, which gives it its shape. The lifting gas is contained in a dozen or more separate cells set inside the framework. The rigid ship would maintain its shape even if all the gas were removed.

The semi-rigid lies between the rigid and non-rigid. It is a pressure ship, but the fabric bag is strengthened by a metal keel, extending the entire length of the ship, with reinforcement at the nose, to prevent this being forced in by air pressure during high-speed flying, and also at the tail where the control surfaces are.

The three classes of ships differ in origin, in size, in construction, and in use. Each has special advantages.

The rigids were born in Germany, although used also in England, America and France. The semi-rigids are built chiefly in

---
*Some authorities recognize two classes only, the pressure airship and the rigid airship (or non-pressure airship). The pressure airship, which would include both the non-rigid and semi-rigid, depends on the internal pressure of its lifting gas for the maintenance of its shape and the withstanding of the stresses imposed upon the ship in flight.

Artist's drawing showing comparative size (starting at left) of non-rigid air yacht; RS-1, Army semi-rigid type ship; the Navy airship Los Angeles and the U. S. S. Akron, being completed by Goodyear-Zeppelin Corp. at Akron for the U. S. Navy.

Norge, Italian ship which made a successful flight to the North Pole.

France and Italy with the latter country more active in recent years in developing this type. The non-rigids have been built in all the countries interested, and were extensively used by the British, French and American naval forces during the war, also by Italy and Germany to some extent.

The rigids are the largest of the three. Since the basic structural form is guaranteed by the rigid framework independent of speed or gas pressure, there is no theoretical limit of size to which the Zeppelin can be built. Engineers may differ as to what is the limiting size in the case of the semi-rigids, but to date no ships of this type approach the dimensions of the Zeppelins. Still smaller sizes are indicated for the non-rigids.

The following table will show this, the figures being the volume in cubic feet of lifting gas:

RIGID AIRSHIPS
American ZRS-4 (under
   construction) 6,500,000
British R-100.............................5,000,000
German Graf Zeppelin................3,700,000
American Los Angeles................2,500,000

SEMI-RIGIDS
Italian Norge................................. 670,000
American RS-1............................. 719,000

NON-RIGIDS
U. S. Army TC-Type.................. 210,000
Navy J Type................................ 210,000
Goodyear Defender...................... 183,000
Goodyear Pilgrim......................... 53,000

The rigid airship is used for long distance operations, primarily over water, where its speed gives it a greater margin of usefulness as compared with steamships.

The semi-rigid may undertake similar functions although its cruising radius will be much less, depending on size and fuel capacity. Designers of this type, however, claim excellent performance efficiency, and certainly the flight of the Italian-built Norge in the Amundsen-Ellsworth-Nobile voyage from Rome to Stolp, East Prussia, to Leningrad, Russia, to Oslo, Norway, to Spitzbergen and from there over the North Pole to Point Barrow and Teller, Alaska, a distance of 6,820 miles, establishes the right of the semi-rigid airship to a respectful hearing.

The smaller non-rigids make no such ambitious claims to long distance flying, although the Naval C-2 flew 2,200 miles from N. Y. (Rockaway Air Station) to Cape Charles Light and returned in 33 hours and 6 minutes, and the C-5 flew from Montauk, L. I., to Cape Race in the same year, a distance of 1,100 miles in 22 hours of rough weather there, and had refueled for an attempt to cross the Atlantic when a 60-mile gale carried it out of the hands of the ground crew and out to sea. The Army C-2 flew from Langley Field, Va., to Ross Field, California, with stops at Akron, Dayton, St. Louis, San An-

Army TC-type ship in use about the time of the World War. Notice the plane it is carrying suspended below the car.

tonio, Nogales and Yuma in 1923, the actual flying time being 67 hours. The Goodyear Defender flew from Akron to Miami with one intermediate stop, 1,240 miles, and smaller Goodyear ships have several times made flights of 500 and 600 miles. The best record in speed perhaps ever made by a non-rigid across country was that of the Puritan, 96,000 cu. ft., piloted by Charles Brannigan, which flew from Akron to Langley Field, Va., in the winter of 1930, making the 425-mile trip in five hours, or better than 80 miles per hour.

Non-rigids were used during the war in coast patrol, submarine reconnaissance, aerial observation, convoy escort, and mine sweeping.

The fact that the non-rigid can be quickly deflated, packed up, shipped across country and reinflated, even in the open, makes it a highly mobile unit. It is useful, too, in observation, air photography, and the direction of artillery fire on a wider front than is possible with anchored kite balloons. In peace time the small ships are used in training officers and crews for the larger ships, in sport, passenger carrying, advertising, and in aerial photography, where they offer a more stable base than the faster airplane. Indeed, the ability of lighter-than-air ships to throttle down and hover over a given spot gives usefulness for certain tasks where the airplane is less effective.

America has experimented with all three types. In rigids with the Shenandoah, whose 9,000-mile flight in 1924 around the rim of the United States stood as the record until the Graf Zeppelin's world flight, and the Los Angeles which has been a successful training and experimental ship, and has, as well, a number of long distance flights over land and water to its credit. These include its 5,500 mile delivery flight from the shops at Friedrichshafen in Central Europe to its new base at Lakehurst, N. J.

The Los Angeles, then in its seventh year, was given a thorough examination in 1930 by a special board which, after exhaustive tests, reported it to be in good condition.

In the semi-rigid field, the Army bought one ship from Italy, the Roma, and built one ship, the RS-1, which was based at Scott Field, Ill., near St. Louis. The Navy also secured an Italian semi-rigid in 1919-20.

The Army and the Navy have maintained a consistent policy of training and research with the non-rigids, particularly at Lakehurst, Langley Field, Va., and Scott Field, Ill., where the smaller craft have built up an enviable performance record.

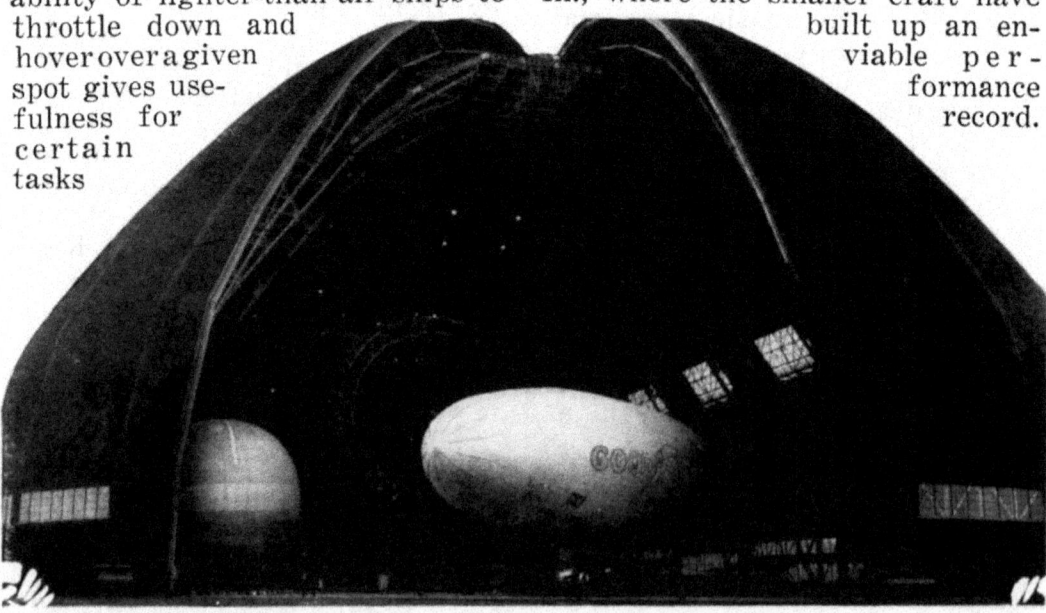

Doors of giant Goodyear-Zeppelin airship dock at Akron partially open and, left to right, may be seen: Goodyear racing balloon, next to it part of the framework of the U. S. S. Akron and at the right one of fleet of six small ships.

CHAPTER IV

The Story of the Zeppelins

COUNT FERDINAND ZEPPELIN, to whose tireless energy and faith the development of airships is chiefly responsible, was born in Constance, July 8, 1838, was graduated from military school and went up through the grades of the German army to major general of cavalry.

It was only after he had retired that he started his real life work, the task that was to make his name internationally famous.

Thirty years before that when the American Civil War was attracting the attention of adventurous young men from all parts of the world, Count Zeppelin, then in his early twenties, came to this country to serve with the Union army as a military observer.

This was to have a profound effect on his life, for at Fort Snelling, Minnesota, and later in Virginia, he had the opportunity to see free and captive balloons in use and to make several ascensions. He was never to forget this experience, and later, during the Franco-Prussian War, when he saw free balloons leaving Paris during the siege, he began seriously to study the possibilities of building motorized balloons or airships.

He tried to interest his government in his ideas as early as 1887,

Hangars and factory of the German Zeppelin Co., the Luftschiffbau-Zeppelin at Friedrichshafen, Germany. Inset: Dr. Hugo Eckener sitting at the window of an airship in flight.

but it was not until 1894, when he was 56 and had retired from active duty, that he completed the design for the first rigid ship. Engineers and public remained unconvinced and the failure of the contemporary Schwartz metal airship experiment a few years later made his task the harder.

In the end, however, in spite of many difficulties, Count Zeppelin succeeded in enlisting the necessary capital to finance his venture; and on July 2, 1900, the first Zeppelin took the air, despite the predictions of the crowds gathered to witness the event.

The Bodensee, an 800,000-cubic-foot ship which started a passenger line to Berlin, carrying 2,380 passengers, making 103 flights in 98 days.

This first ship, 419 feet long and with two 16 H. P. motors, succeeded on its third flight in reaching a speed of 18 miles per hour. Though Count Zeppelin felt that the demonstration had been a success, he realized the need of a larger, stronger ship with more powerful motors. It took him five years this time to raise the money. In 1905, however, the King of Wurttemberg and an aluminum manufacturer backed him on his second ship. The new Zeppelin rose to 1,640 feet but was forced to land because of motor trouble, and a winter storm wrecked it before it could be flown back to its hangar.

This convinced everyone, except Count Zeppelin himself, that airships were impractical. The aged inventor, then 68, threw himself and the last of his resources into the task of building a third ship, completing it late in 1906. This ship was immediately successful. The German government became interested and announced its willingness to buy a ship if it could remain aloft for a 24-hour period.

So Zeppelin built his fourth ship, one-fifth the size of the present-day Los Angeles, and on its first trip flew it over the Alps to Lucerne and back. This feat aroused enthusiasm all over Germany and the official duration flight was arranged. The rejoicing was premature, for the airship motors of that day had not reached the stage of dependability that exists today. Engine trouble compelled a forced landing, a storm blew up before his engines were repaired, the ship got out of control of the emergency ground crew and was wrecked.

This disaster would have broken the spirit of most men. But Zeppelin carried his case to the people. The response was overwhelming. The carpenter, the farmer, the storekeeper, the postman, the mechanic, the school-teacher put their contributions at his disposal, gave him a vote of confidence as inspiring as ever came to any inventor at the moment of disaster. A total of 6,000,000 marks (about $1,250,000) was subscribed. The Count was so touched by this result that he placed the money in trust, founding the "Zeppelin Endowment for the Propagation of Air Navigation" which today controls the Luftschiffbau-Zeppelin, the building company, and other subsidiaries and which has in its charter the provision that profits were to go back into the cause of aeronautics.

One result of this was that, as the Foundation became rich and powerful, it invested its earnings in expansion, producing its own motors at one subsidiary, airplanes at another, had its own gear works, hangar building company, its own commercial operating company, carried on great research activities.

Count Zeppelin had the gift of attracting clever young men to his standard. He uncovered a motor-building genius in Karl Maybach and his airship troubles were well behind him once he got a dependable engine.

He started Claude Dornier building metal flying boats, which were to be precursors to the great Dornier DO-X of today. He found a great designer in Arnstein, a constructor in Duerr, an executive in Lehmann, a financier in Colsman. In converting to the Zeppelin cause Hugo Eckener, journalist, economist and Zeppelin critic, he uncovered a man destined to become the greatest of Zeppelin captains and eventually the old Count's successor.

Dr. Eckener was given charge of Delag, the passenger-carrying subsidiary, as his first important assignment.

A number of passenger airships were built for Delag, terminals set up at various points over Germany, bookings were arranged through the Hamburg-American Lines; and in three years more than 35,000 passengers were carried over various routes.

Six ships were in service, the Schwaben, Sachsen, Viktoria Luise, Deutschland I and II and the Hansa and hangars had been erected either by the Zeppelin company, Delag, or municipalities at Berlin, Baden-Baden, Dusseldorf, Frankfurt a. M., Hamburg, Leipzig and Dresden.

Then the war came. Military officials had high expectations regarding the fighting qualities of the big airships. Many Zeppelins were built, first for the army, then the navy. The ships became larger and more efficient as the grim battle in France wore on. Designs were changed, and changed again to meet war needs. At one time speed was stressed, then cruising range, then the ability to climb to altitudes where they could not be pursued by speedy planes. Hulls were strengthened and made more rigid, yet lighter; machine guns were mounted at points of vantage and bomb-dropping apparatus perfected. An observation car was developed which could be suspended 3,000 feet below the ship by a slender cable which also acted as a telephone line, so that an observer, riding in the tiny sky gondola, a mere speck in the sky, could direct the navigating and fighting operations of the ship, itself invisible in clouds overhead.

Dr. Arnstein, one of the keenest mathematicians of Europe, called away at the outbreak of war from such tasks as building high arched bridges in the Alps and rebuilding the Cathedral at Strassburg applied scientific principles of these analysis and aerodynamics brought into the airship industry, became chief engineer within a year, built 68 ships before the war ended.

Zeppelin ships flew several millions of miles during the war in conjunction with the fleet, in patrol, reconnaissance, mine-sweeping and bombing operations.

During the war period, Luftschiffbau-Zeppelin designed and built 88 airships at its four construction docks, making a total of 115 built from 1900 through to 1918. Count Zeppelin himself died in 1917. He did not live to carry out his ambition to create passenger lines over the continent and to America.

The Zeppelin company resumed operations after the war, building the Bodensee, of 800,000 cu. ft. capacity, but with twice the speed and efficiency of pre-war commercial airships, started a passenger line to Berlin, carrying 2,380 passengers, making 103 flights in 98 days and was completing a second ship, the Nordstern, when the Inter-Allied Air Commission stepped in, took over the ships, assigned them to France and Italy, forbade all further operations. It was due to this circumstance that the Zeppelin company's accumulated experience in building and flying airships became available to America in 1924.

1. Graf Zeppelin moored at Los Angeles airport with a small non-rigid airship flying above it. 2. Cleveland air races honor Dr. Eckener at conclusion of his round-the-world flight; left to right: Fred M. Harpham, vice president of Goodyear; former Commander J. C. Hunsaker, vice president of the Goodyear-Zeppelin Corp. and president of the Pacific Zeppelin Company; P. W. Litchfield (hat in hand), president of the Goodyear Companies; Dr. Hugo Eckener, commander of the Graf Zeppelin; Dr. Karl Arnstein (wearing glasses), vice president of the Goodyear-Zeppelin Corp. in charge of design. 3. Airship Defender at Eckener celebration at Cleveland airport. Notice shadow of another of the airship fleet in background. 4. Home of the Graf Zeppelin, airship hangar of the Luftschiffbau-Zeppelin in Friedrichshafen, Germany.

CHAPTER V

Goodyear in Aeronautics

GOODYEAR'S lighter-than-air craft activity began in 1911. Zeppelin ships and Wright airplanes were beginning to demonstrate the two great principles of flight. The company was already in the business of impregnating fabric with rubber. Looking ahead, a market was seen in airship covers and airplane wings. And though rubberized wings, in the case of airplanes, were to be superseded by wings of doped fabric, the business in lighter-than-air craft was to grow to large proportions.

Goodyear built its first balloon in 1912 and many flights were made around Akron. It was Mr. Litchfield's theory that a company could best find out how to build better balloons by flying them.

In 1913 a Goodyear balloon was entered in the James Gordon Bennett international race, which was started from Paris. There was a large field of entries from many nations. The wind carried the contestants westward toward the Atlantic ocean. All landed except one. Upson and Preston, the Americans, went out to sea, calculating from the weather reports to find a wind later that would carry them back to England. Their observations were correct, they landed in England and won the

Dr. Karl Arnstein, vice president in charge of engineering of Goodyear-Zeppelin Corp., who has built 70 rigid airships.

race, the first of many victories by Goodyear balloonists.

Aeronautical activities grew at Akron and when the war came the company began building training balloons, kite balloons, and airships on a large scale. The problem of training arose and Wingfoot Lake air station, 10 miles from the factory, was established. A great hangar, 400x100x100, was built, a hydrogen plant, shops, barracks. Goodyear balloonists were set to work assembling ships, training army and navy officers.

Group of free balloons used for war-time training of lighter-than-air pilots at Goodyear airship dock at Wingfoot Lake Station near Akron.

"Walking" one of the earlier type T. C. ships from its construction dock at Wingfoot Lake.

More than 600 men were trained there, went out to coastal air stations extending from Panama to Cape Cod and skirting the Bay of Biscay. Great swaying kite balloons were led out of the shops to be used in France for aerial observation and direction of artillery fire. Goodyear airships were flown cross country to Atlantic bases, to be used in coast patrols and anti-submarine defense, were packed up and shipped to France.

At the peak of the war period some 2,000 men and girls were at work in the balloon room and Goodyear was building more balloons each month than one of the leading allied nations turned out in four years of war.

In that period upwards of 1,000 balloons were built and delivered, close to 100 non-rigid airships to the United States, England and France.

Construction activities continued after the war, though at lessened tension. In 1924 the RS-1, first semi-rigid ship to be built in America, left Akron for assembly at Scott Field. The gas cells for the Shenandoah were also built there.

The year 1924, delivery year of the airship Los Angeles, saw the acquiring of the Zeppelin patents, an important step not merely for Goodyear, but for America. Germany lay under interdict of the allies against building of aircraft lest new military weapons be forged. With the dismantling then projected of the huge Zeppelin hangars on Lake Constance, the great organization which the genius of Count Zeppelin and his associates had created seemed doomed to pass out of existence and the art of airship building destroyed.

It was in this emergency that the Goodyear company stepped in, brought the Zeppelin rights and patents to America. A subsidiary, the Goodyear-Zeppelin Corporation, was organized into which all of Goodyear's lighter-than-air business, personnel and patents were thrown to add to the German experience, making a most impressive accumulation of engineering knowledge.

Dr. Karl Arnstein, chief engineer of Luftschiffbau-Zeppelin during the time it was building some 70 rigid airships, joined the company with 12 of his technical experts, taking the title of vice president in charge of engineering.

The new corporation set to work at once, after its organization, studying matters of material, supply, helium, hangars and operating bases, began initial design of ships which it foresaw would shortly be called for.

When the United States Navy awarded it the contract for two American airships, the Goodyear-Zeppelin Corporation was prepared to start immediately with the erection of a construction dock or hangar and the fabrication of the ZRS-4, later named the "Akron."

During this period, former Commander J. C. Hunsaker (C. C.), U. S. Navy, who had been in charge of aircraft design for the Navy during the war, became a vice president of the corporation, to develop the project of airship lines crossing the two oceans, which were to result in 1929 in the organization of the Pacific-Zeppelin Transport Corporation and the International Zeppelin Transport Corporation.

CHAPTER VI

The Free Balloon

THE free balloon belongs properly in a discussion of airships inasmuch as it is the primary training craft for airship crews.

For the airship is substantially a motorized free balloon, shaped to give it directability. The contraction and expansion of lifting gases with variances in altitude or temperature, the problems of handling of large masses in flight, are similar. The dirigible pilot must first study free ballooning. If motors should fail in an airship it becomes a free balloon.

Sensitive to air conditions, the balloon furnishes its pilots with valuable information about weather and becomes itself an important factor in the study of meteorology.

The balloon drifts with the wind, may merely be sent aloft or brought down at the will of the pilot. So that the public usually does not realize the fact that there is a science to ballooning, and that to get maximum distance on a balloon flight involves the most careful study of the weather, and the most skillful search for favoring

An 80,000 cubic foot capacity racing balloon being inflated prior to take-off in International Race. Notice one of the non-rigid airships flying above. Below: Giant mushrooms—balloons entered in National Balloon Race, Houston, Texas, July 4, 1930.

winds—a search which must be made at the expense of either ballast or lifting gas.

A balloon race for distance represents the highest test of a pilot's skill, knowledge and courage. An international balloon race has been held every year since 1906, except the war years, for the James Gordon Bennett trophy. The American contestants are selected by an elimination race for which the P. W. Litchfield Trophy is the award. Army, navy and civilians contest annually for a place on the American team.

There are many colorful chapters in the history of balloon racing. Upson's flight across the English Channel was the first that had been made since that of Jeffries and Blanchard in 1786, though the Channel has been crossed many times since. The Great Lakes in this country have been crossed and recrossed. Van Orman flew across the Baltic into Sweden in 1925 to win the James Gordon Bennett Trophy, and Lt. Settle crossed the Gulf of St. Lawrence, landing on Prince Edward Island to win the national race in 1929.

1. Ward T. Van Orman, Goodyear balloon pilot, winner of three international races and five national balloon races, with Alan MacCracken, co-pilot, in the basket of Goodyear VIII taking off in a National Race. 2. Just before the take-off. 3. Air view of balloons being made ready for National Race starting from Bettes Field, Pittsburgh.

The Hawley-Post flight of 1910 from St. Louis to the woods of Quebec province, where they were lost from civilization for nearly two weeks; the landing of Van Orman on the deck of a ship 60 miles off Brest; Bienaime's 1,300-mile flight from Paris to Moscow in 1912 are among the many colorful incidents in the history of balloon racing. In this history Goodyear balloonists played a conspicuous role.

The flying of balloons in order to learn how to improve them was a specified duty of airship engineers. Out of this circumstance there developed a group of pilots who have had conspicuous success in balloon racing, having won nine national races and three international events.

A resume of balloon racing is printed in the appendix.

Parade of six Akron non-rigid commercial ships.

CHAPTER VII

Blimps or Air Yachts

AN UNUSUAL chapter in the story of the airship is that of the first privately operated ships. The Goodyear company built its first ship in 1919, a tiny hydrogen bag of 37,000 cubic feet, just one one-hundredth the size of the Graf Zeppelin and nicknamed the Pony Blimp. Based in Los Angeles alongside the company's rubber factory there, it gave a colorful demonstration in the next few years of the possibilities of small aircraft. It was employed in passenger carrying between Los Angeles and Catalina Islands, in mapping deep sea fishing, and in motion picture making.

For while the airplane had become by then a common sight, the only lighter-than-air craft were the army and navy airships, rarely seen by the public and then at a distance. The Goodyear "blimps" could come down out of the sky and mix with the people of America.

In 1925 the company began building a fleet of small airships to be used for experimental purposes and to train pilots for later Zeppelins. The fleet soon gave striking demonstrations of the usefulness of this division of aircraft.

The present Goodyear fleet began with the Pilgrim, a 51,000-cubic-foot capacity ship. It was called "America's first air yacht," as the first non-rigid to be built with a closed cabin. It was flown with the non-inflammable helium gas, as were the others from then on.

In 1928 came the Puritan, a twin-motored cabin ship of 86,000 cubic feet (enlarged later on to 96,000). It set off immediately on

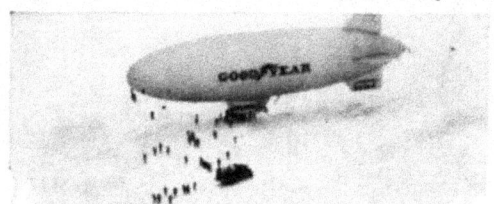

Winter flying. Airship Defender at Akron Municipal Airport.

a demonstration tour, flew 8,000 miles in the next 60 days, carried 600 passengers.

Early in 1929 the Volunteer, Mayflower, and Vigilant of the Puritan type came out of the shop, and lastly the Defender, flagship, 184 feet long and with a gas capacity of 186,000 cubic feet, capable of carrying 10 passengers.

The Pilgrim uses a 60 h. p. Lawrence radial motor, the Vigilant, Volunteer and Mayflower have two 82 h. p. Siemens-Halske motors, the Puritan two 110 h. p. Warners, and the Defender a pair of 165 h. p. Wright Whirlwinds.

In naming the ships, President Litchfield selected names made famous by the American cup defenders in international yachting. Since the non-rigid ships were to serve a similar purpose for persons living inland as do yachts for those living along the seacoast this selection seemed appropriate.

The Volunteer, after completion, was sent to California, to be based at Los Angeles. The Mayflower went to New Bedford, Mass., where it spent the four months at an airport on the estate of Col. E. H. R. Greene, being used in experimental flights in co-operation with radio

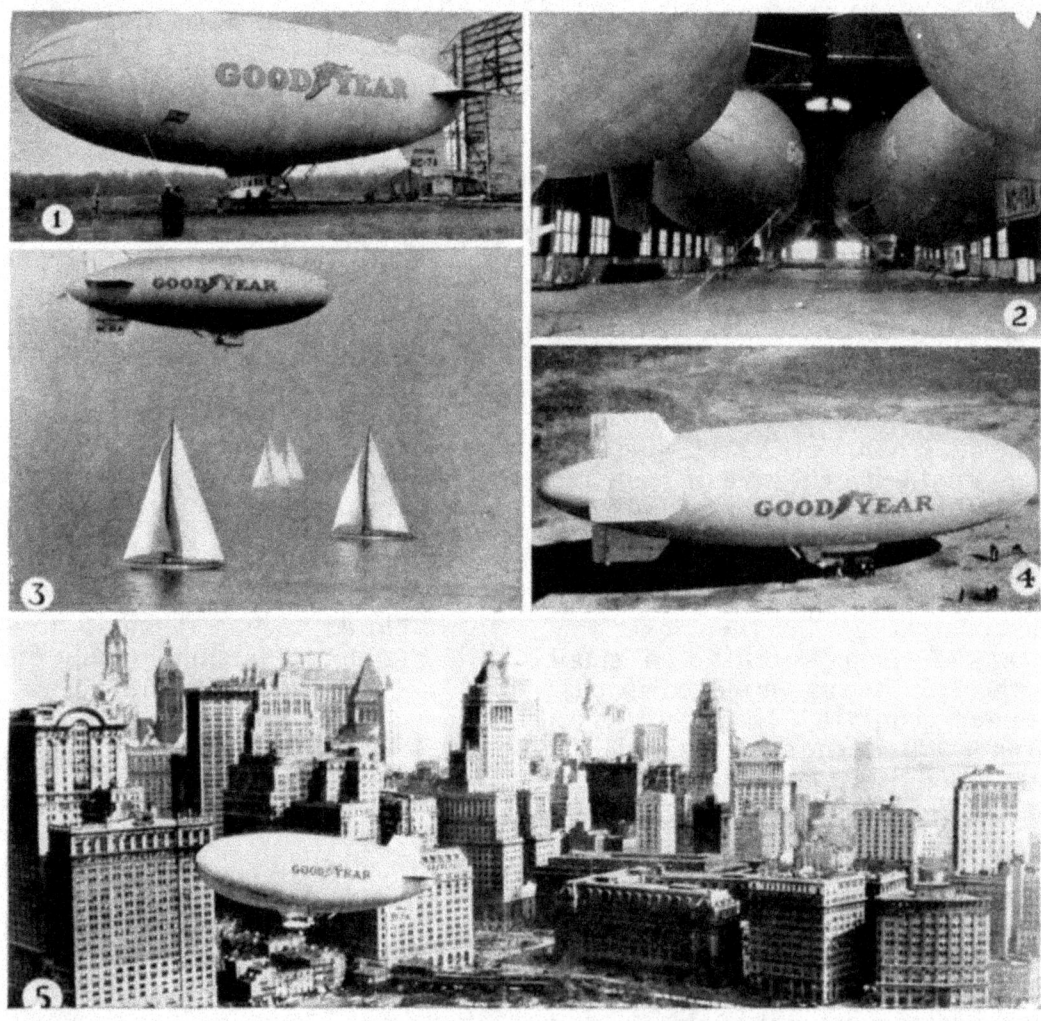

1. Airship Puritan leaving dock at Wingfoot Lake. 2. In for the night. Unusual view of six of Goodyear fleet berthed in the Wingfoot Lake dock. 3. Airship Mayflower took part in International Yacht Races in 1930. The ship carried a broadcasting outfit and the races were thus described and relayed to the nation. 4. Airship Defender on commercial operation flying passengers. 5. Airship Puritan visits New York City and flies over the Battery.

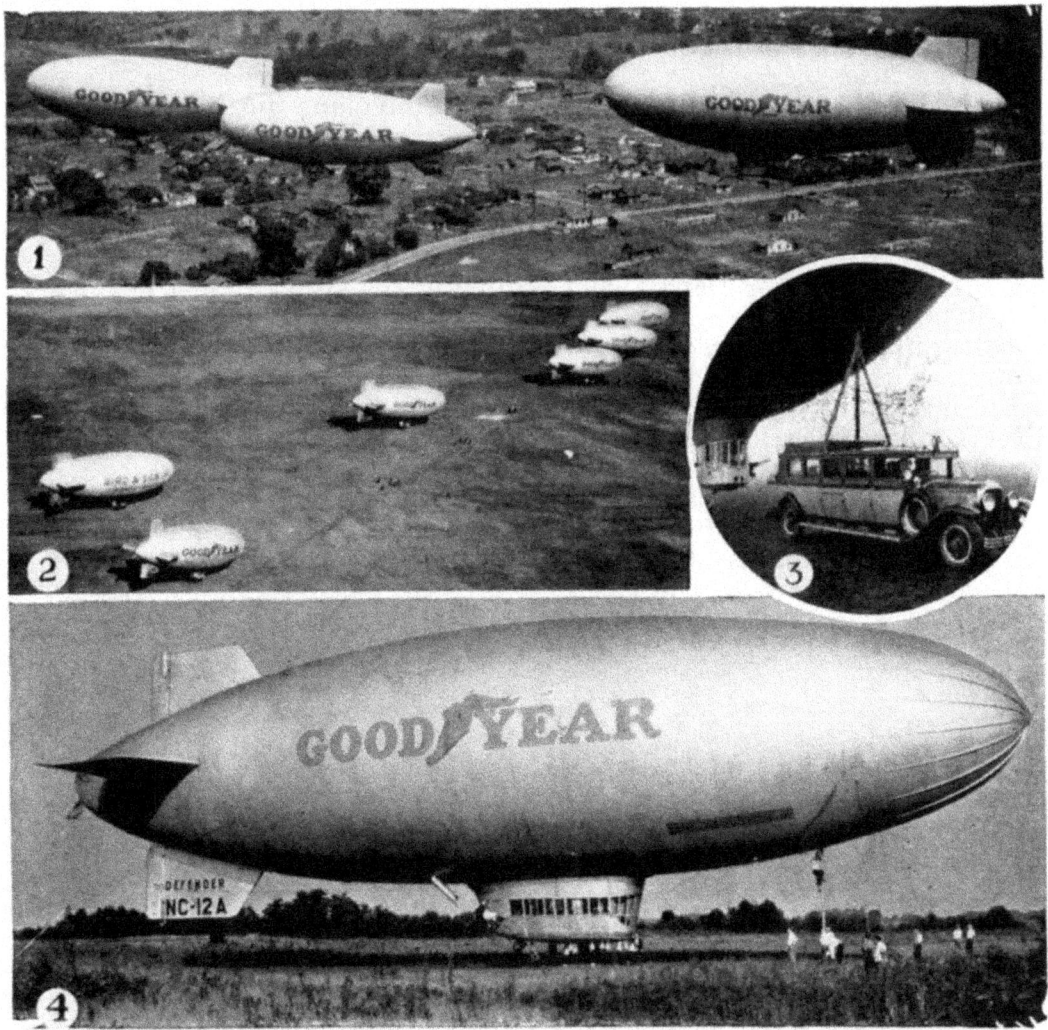

1. Close-up of three non-rigid airships flying in formation. 2. Parade rest. Six airships of Akron fleet taxiing into position for military inspection. 3. Portable mooring mast used for overnight masting when ship is on operations too far away to return to its dock at night. The bus transports the ship's landing crew as well. When not in use the mast is folded down and strapped to the top of the bus. 4. Stub mast sometimes used in operations. Note the man near the top securing the ship.

research scientists of the Massachusetts Institute of Technology. Basing at government hangars at Lakehurst, N. J., Aberdeen, Md., Langley Field, Va., Pensacola, Fla., and Scott Field, Ill., at a private hangar at Detroit, and municipal docks at Miami and St. Petersburg during the winter, the eastern ships carried on demonstrations during 1929-30 that covered every state east of the Mississippi except Wisconsin and Maine, and included trips to Toronto and Havana. The Volunteer carried on similar flights along the Pacific coast as far north as Sacramento and south to the Mexican border.

During the winter of 1930-31 it was decided to enlarge three of the fleet—the Volunteer, the Mayflower and the Vigilant. The Volunteer was increased to 96,000 cubic feet capacity. The Mayflower and the Vigilant to 112,000 cubic feet, and their cabins enlarged to accommodate six passengers. The Vigilant was renamed the Columbia.

A new airship dock, large enough to accommodate the Defender, was begun at Holmes airport, New York City, in the spring of 1931, to provide a base for passenger operations in the metropolitan area, and negotiations were begun for similar bases in Chicago and other cities.

Up to May 1, 1931, the Goodyear fleet had flown 596,600 miles, had carried 43,395 passengers, had made 18,722 flights. During these flights the fleet performed important training service for some 25 men who qualified for Department of Commerce licenses and from whose ranks officer personnel for future air lines may be chosen.

An important improvement in ship handling developed through the small ships is the taxi wheel, actually a balloon airplane tire swiveled under the cabin. Using this even the smaller Goodyear ships may start a cross-country trip with half a ton overload of gasoline, taxi across the airport like an airplane until it gets flying speed, then take off. It can carry more than it can lift.

Another was the portable mooring mast attached to the roof of the bus used by the ground crew, permitting the ship to mast out overnight at places where no hangar is available, and useful also in taking a ship in and out of the hangar in cross winds. The mast can also be set up in half an hour on an airport or open field. Outriggers with small balloon tires at the ends were added to the bus mast to hold it against side gusts.

1. Defender over Cuban capitol building at Havana. 2. Col. Charles A. Lindbergh and Mrs. Lindbergh, passengers in Goodyear ship Volunteer. 3. Outrigger equipped portable mooring mast. 4. Interior cabin of Defender. 5. U. S. Navy dirigible J-4 at Holmes airport, Jackson Heights, L. I., ground breaking ceremonies. Goodyear Defender operates from this base in summer.

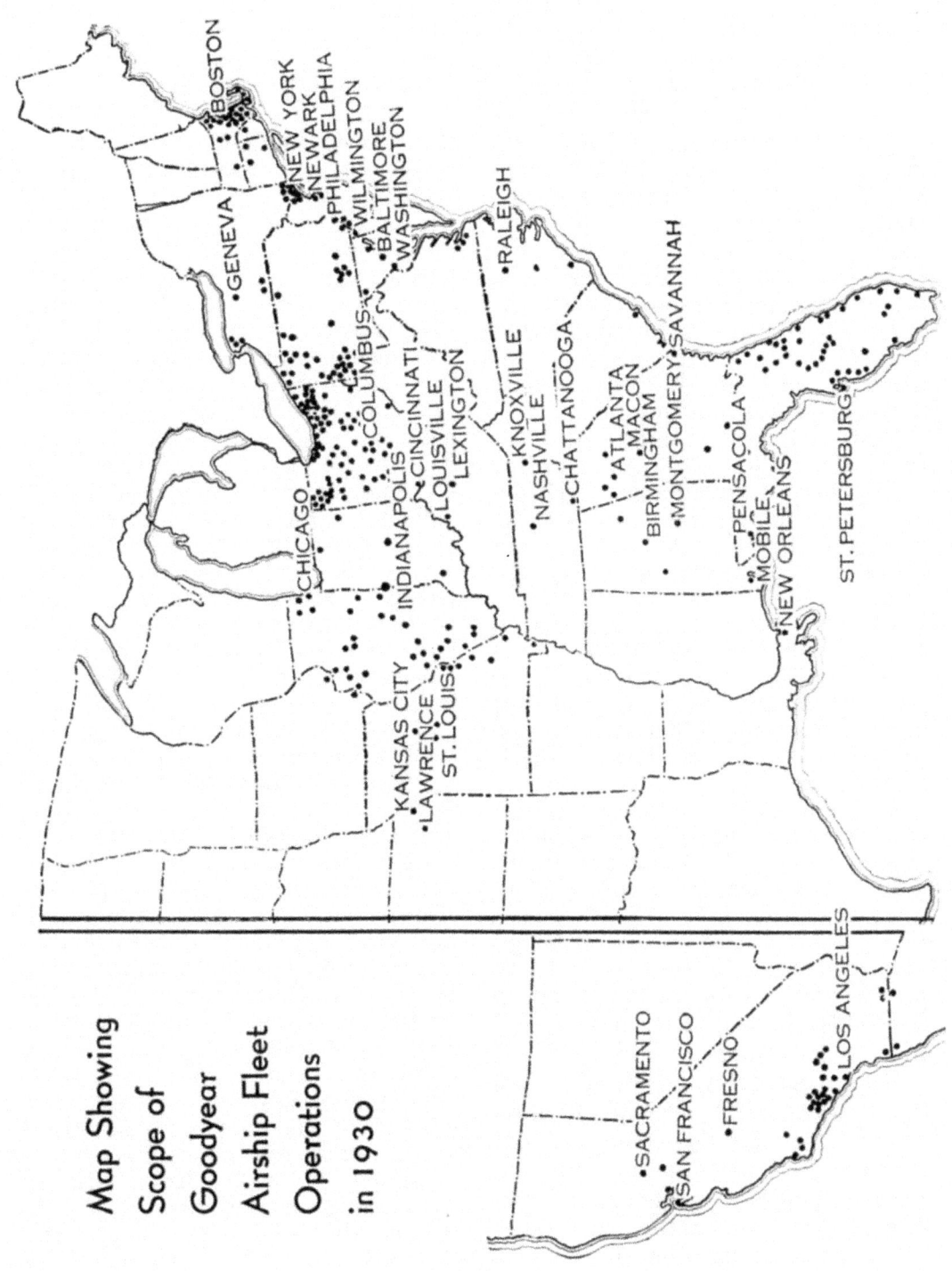

CHAPTER VIII

Planning for the Naval Ships

WITH great areas of land to fly over, with great distances separating it from Europe and the Orient, with the accumulated experience of this country and Europe to draw on, with engineering and financial resources with exclusive possession of helium, it was natural for America to become interested in the lighter-than-air division of aeronautics.

Rear Admiral William A. Moffett, Chief of the Bureau of Aeronautics, recommended the securing of additional ships of the rigid type for the Navy. He found Congress interested and responsive.

In June, 1926, the construction of two ships of 6,500,000-cubic-foot capacity was authorized, as part of a five-year program of aeronautic development which grew out of the Morrow committee's study.

Decision had to be made whether the construction of the airships should be done by the Navy itself.

The Navy was well equipped to undertake the task. Its engineers had made intensive study of design and operation for years, had collected every scrap of information available, had had access to the files of the allied nations.

Their association with the British had been particularly close during the period that Great Britain was most active in this field. Commander Zachary Lansdowne, U. S. N., then assistant naval attache, flew on the British R-34 as the official American observer on the transatlantic crossing of 1919.

The Navy had had invaluable experience in actual designing, building and flying a successful airship in the case of the Shenandoah. Its engineers were also conversant with the German methods through the accession of the German-built Los Angeles. An inspection force, headed by Commander Garland Fulton, Construction Corps, U. S. N., had been stationed at Friedrichshafen during the whole period of construction of the Los Angeles, acting as representatives of the United States government. Under Navy command the Los Angeles had had a longer operating experience than any airship ever built.

The Navy had completed preliminary designs for a modern airship. It could be fabricated at the Naval Aircraft Factory at Philadelphia and assembled at Lakehurst as was done in the case of the Shenandoah.

However, it seemed desirable for America to have an airship building industry, as it had a shipbuilding industry for surface craft. The World War had indicated the necessity of industrial preparedness, along with military. Such establishments having plants, specialized machinery and experienced personnel, are properly considered a secondary line of defense. The existence of a building industry for airships might, as well, lead to the establishment of commercial airlines, whose ships, terminals

U. S. S. Los Angeles, Navy J-type ships, captive balloon and five navy free balloons.

Nose view of U. S. S. Los Angeles, being towed from hangar by mobile mast.

and personnel would also be available to the country in emergency.

This was in line with government policy. There was a time, for example, when armor plate for battleships was all imported from abroad. The Navy Department thought it important to have a source of supply in this country, drew up detailed specifications, induced American iron mills to undertake the manufacture of battleship steel—and so helped lay the foundation for the steel industry in this country. Similarly, the establishment of chemical and other industries were appreciably helped by government support.

Taking all such considerations into account, the Navy instituted a design contest, drawing on its accumulation of experience to set up specifications as to strength, safety and the like, more complete than had ever been issued on airships. The specifications directed the attention of contestants to the possibilities of definite improvements in design as against past practice.

A total of 37 designs was submitted. First place was awarded to the Goodyear-Zeppelin Corporation in a decision announced in July, 1927.

Congress had appropriated $200,000 to start construction on the first ship. In July, 1928, funds were made available. An Eastern corporation, however, with experience in building surface ships, became interested, asked for an opportunity to submit designs, so the competition was reopened. This time Goodyear-Zeppelin submitted three alternative designs, and in a decision announced by the Navy in August, 1928, was awarded first, second and third places. In October, 1928, formal award of the contract was made to the Goodyear-Zeppelin Corporation.

Work was started at once on a huge airship factory and dock in Akron, which was completed in December, 1929. Construction and testing of the first ring girder started simultaneously in the shop and actual assembly of the ZRS-4, first of the two ships, was formally started November 7, 1929, when Rear Admiral Moffet drove a golden rivet into the master ring.

The first ship was scheduled for completion in 1931, the second one 15 months later. The two ships were designated the ZRS-4 and the ZRS-5. The name "The Akron" was given in 1930 to the ZRS-4 by Secretary of the Navy Charles Francis Adams.

CHAPTER IX

Building the Airship Dock

THE dock or hangar in which "The Akron" is being constructed, at Akron airport two miles from the Goodyear factory, half a mile from the Goodyear-Zeppelin shops, is the largest and perhaps the most unusual building of its kind in the world.

As a piece of engineering it is little less interesting than the airships to be built under its massive dome, and so has attracted hundreds of thousands of visitors.

One delicate part of airship operation is that of taking the ship in and out of the dock in a cross wind. So it is important that the building should cause the least practical interference with wind currents in order that these operations may not be complicated by cross currents created by the building itself, or by the open doors.

It was this consideration which, after elaborate wind tunnel tests, conducted at the Guggenheim School of Aeronautics, New York University, and elsewhere confirmed the judgment of Dr. Arnstein, who, with his staff, developed the basic design in fixing the shape of the structure—approximately a semi-paraboloid.

The orange-peel-shaped doors, weighing 600 tons each, follow the contour of the building in opening and closing and are attached to a single six-foot pin at the top and roll on 40 wheels, assembled on four-wheel trucks, riding on a circular track.

The building is 1,175 feet long 325 feet wide, and 211 feet high, the largest structure in the world without interior support. Seven football games might be played simultaneously under its roof, six miles of standard railroad tracks could be laid on its eight and one-half acres of floor, 100,000 people could gather within its walls, the Lexington and Saratoga, the great airplane carriers, could be housed there, the Woolworth building could be laid lengthwise inside and the Washington monument added alongside it and there would still be ample room.

The interior floor area is 364,000 square feet, while the cubical content amounts to 45,000,000 cubic feet. The roof area is 687,000 square feet; more than 23,000 square feet of skylights are used. The structural steel in the four doors weighs 2,400 tons and that in

Photographer shows with two pictures how big dock is 75 feet longer than Niagara Falls (American side).

Three-quarter view of the world's largest airship dock of the Goodyear-Zeppelin Corp. at Akron, Ohio, where the U. S. S. Akron was built. The doors which slide around the sides of the building are slightly open.

the shell and shops 4,800 tons, making a total of 7,200 tons.

Tunnels have been built under the concrete floors for service facilities and for the docking rails, which will be used for moving the ships in and out of the structure. All service facilities, power, light, water, helium gas are brought into the building underground.

Since the 7,200 tons of steel in the framework expand and contract with changes in temperature, the arches of the building are placed on rollers, so that the giant building may be said literally to breathe.

Several working platforms, lowered from the roof, give the workmen access to the ship; and a series of six catwalks along the under side of the curving roof make the upper reaches accessible. An inclined railway, the cars being counterbalanced, carries the workmen to their stations aloft.

In erecting the great arches of the building, the two curving sides were erected first, the center top arch was assembled on the floor and hoisted into position by cranes and counterweights. So exactly had the work been estimated that each center arch fitted exactly and needed only to be riveted into place.

There are many interesting details in connection with the building. For example, the great hinge pins at the top of each end of the building which hold the doors, one pin for each door.

These pins, six feet long, 17 inches in diameter, do not have to hold the weight of the door since these rest on the wheel trucks at the base. They do have to be strong enough to keep the door from being pushed outward when a strong wind is blowing through the building and have to resist any sideways pressure on the part of the door on account of wind or snow.

The pin, although tons of metal are used to make it fast, is not in a fixed position, as the sun's heat causes expansion and contraction that will move the entire roof and wobble the pin around several inches. To provide for this movement, the horizontal thrust bearing is made a ball and socket joint.

There was a problem of wear on the wheels supporting the door. The outer wheels travel further than the inner ones when the door is opening or closing which would slip one wheel continuously. So each wheel is separately housed and each pair is set radially so as not to bind against the rails.

Again, the doors must be under control at all times, must not be able to start off by themselves, swinging around in a heavy wind.

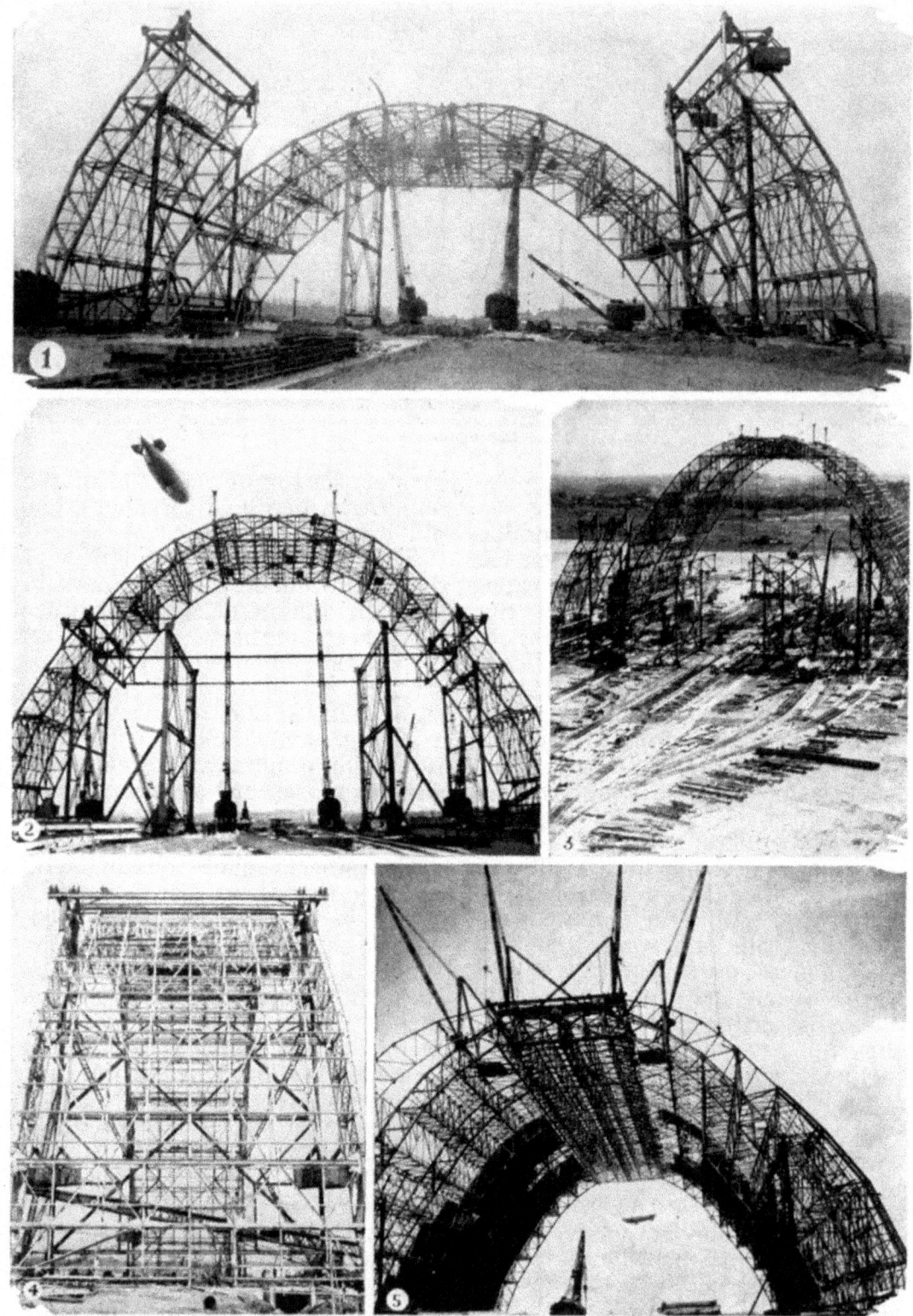

Steps in the construction of the airship dock at Akron. 1. Erection of first arch of framework. Center section raised and placed on haunch sections at sides. 2. First arch in place. 3. Construction of second arch. 4. This mass of steelwork is an end view of one arch. 5. Intricate steelwork of roof with covering partially on.

1. U. S. Navy ship Los Angeles flying over the dock at the ring laying ceremonies in November, 1929. Framework of dock doors may be seen here. 2. Ground view progress picture showing growth of airship dock. 3. Looking through the door framework. 4. Doors of the dock, weighing 1,200 tons to the pair, are mounted on standard railway trucks. Door framework here on trucks is ready for outside covering. 5. View along the top of the dock. Small dots in distance are men.

Completed dock with doors partially open. Observe the automobiles parked alongside the building.

A "rack drive" system was devised, with a large "bull gear" with great coarse teeth mounted on a fixed concrete base outside the building at each corner. The gear engages a rack which is attached rigidly to the door itself. Thus, as the motor revolves the bull gear turns slowly and the rack is driven back and forth, pushing the door with it. Worm gear reduction was used because of its characteristic of being "self locking."

The doors can be driven at as high as 40 feet a minute, but automatically slow down to a creeping speed as the doors come to wide open or closed position. Stops are automatic.

The building was so large that it seemed useless to attempt to heat it except in offices and shops. Portable electric heaters were devised for working platforms in cold weather. Only a relatively small amount of natural light is provided, as the ship assembly proceeds night and day artificial light is necessary anyhow for close work.

Adjustable projectors of 1,000-watt lights are located along the catwalks at levels of 65 feet up to 150 feet.

Roofing was a problem. Wood was out of the question on account of the fire hazard. The roof must also be water tight, provide maximum insulation and must meet strength requirements of 200 pounds per square foot on the upper half, 100 pounds per square foot on the lower half.

A helium storage plant was built underground, alongside the dock, huge cylinders having a total capacity of more than 1,000,000 cubic feet of gas at 750 pounds pressure, being utilized. The gas will be drawn by suction from

Side view of structure, in which seven football games could be played simultaneously.

storage tanks to gas cells or vice versa at the rate of 1,000,000 cubic feet in 24 hours, or can be removed at a somewhat slower rate for purification.

Preparation of the site for the dock required removal of 1,000,000 cubic yards of earth. Nearly 1,300 concrete piles were driven to rock as a base for the structure, each pile being able to stand a weight of 30 tons.

Previously the largest hangars were those at Lakehurst, N. J., and Belleville, Ill., American navy and army lighter-than-air bases, the Zeppelin hangars at Friedrichshafen and Potsdam, the French hangar at Orly, the British sheds at Cardington, Howden and Pulham, England, and at Karachi, India.

The building cost close to two and a quarter million dollars and required eleven months to build. Actual erection of steel started April 29, 1929, the north doors being completed on Nov. 25, as the last important part of the construction job.

Interior view of dock just after completion and before work on the giant Navy aircraft was begun.

Inset: "Believe it or not," by Ripley, commented upon the fact that so vast is the area of this dock (eight and a half acres under roof) that it has its own clouds and condensations of moisture. Read what Ripley says in his cartoon.

CHAPTER X

Improvements in Airship Design

THOUGH Montgolfier had proved as early as the 18th century that a gas-filled balloon would go aloft and Giffard, 60 years later, that its movements in air could be directed, demonstration of the airship as a practical carrier was to wait for the internal combustion engine and the sturdy, light-weight metal, duralumin.

Granted that such a ship would fly, it must be strong enough to withstand gales and rough landings, must carry motive power enough to outfly storms or buck its way through head winds, must carry fuel enough to give it broad cruising radius.

All these are costly in weight, and in a vehicle where every added pound made it necessary to enlarge proportionately the size of the balloon section where the gas was carried, light-weight motors and metal were essential.

One of Count Zeppelin's greatest contributions to aeronautics was the courage and intelligence that dictated his decision to get the necessary motive power, fuel capacity, and structural strength by building his ships completely reinforced with metal framework, regardless of what that cost in weight.

Previous ships had kept their shape, only through the gas pressure within, as the non-rigids do today. And to get the gas capacity to carry even the metal skeletons of the ships themselves, Zeppelin had to go to sizes that seemed to his day to be not merely impracticable but visionary. As a practical matter, too, he multiplied his problems, since his great ships needed large crews to fly or land them, needed large hangars and docks, needed large capital expenditures before they could be built at all.

With scarce twenty years elapsing since the airship principle was definitely accepted and with a total of less than 160 rigid airships built so far in the whole world, the wonder remains not that airships

Artist's conception of how the U. S. S. Akron will look passing over the nation's Capitol.

32

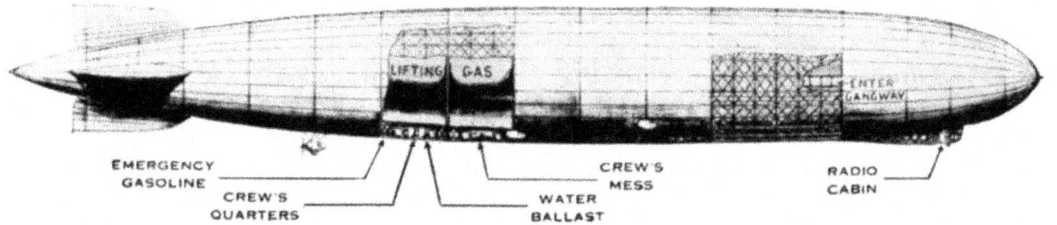

Cut-away drawing of the Graf Zeppelin, showing some of the ship's construction and where various functions are located.

have not come into their own earlier, but that so much progress has been made at all.

Not only in Germany but in England, America and France, engineers have studied the improvements of airships and have contributed to the art. Scores of improvements have been made in design, in motors, in communication systems, in stress calculations, in materials.

England gave the world the mooring mast, the late Major G. H. Scott being assigned the major part of the credit for it. America added so much to the simplifying of mooring and handling operations that a special chapter must be given to that. Maybach in Germany, Packard and others in America, Rolls-Royce and Beardmore in England built better and better engines. Reversing motors were perfected, giving better control in landing.

America contributed helium gas as a factor of vital importance in safety. The ballast recovery device developed in this country and the use of Blau gas in the Graf Zeppelin, both important improvements, will be discussed in the following chapter.

In various quarters men are experimenting with oil-burning engines, with Diesels, with the use of hydrogen itself as fuel, or with various fuels of different weights in alternation.

The search for improvement has gone into the basic materials of construction. Here's one example: The cells, which contain the lifting gas, have to date been made of gold beater skin, laid down in two plies on thin cotton fabric.

Now, gold beater skin is merely a small section of the intestines of a steer, used since the Middle Ages by goldsmiths for the hammering out of golf leaf because of its thinness and extraordinary strength. Gold beater skin from 400,000 cattle went into the gas cells of the Los Angeles, each one laid by hand and with meticulous precision.

So a great deal of research went into the matter of finding a substitute which would avoid the vast amount of hand labor. Two were evolved at the Goodyear laboratories: one a rubberized fabric which while slightly heavier had satisfactory impermeability and was less expensive to make up and easier to handle; the other a gelatine latex fabric in which many coats of latex and gelatine were spread over fabric, and which matched the gold beater skin in weight and showed considerably higher resistance to gas diffusion.

Test cells were made up for the Los Angeles and proved so satisfactory that they were specified for the Akron, half the cells to be rubberized fabric, the other half gelatine latex.

In like manner British airship designers used non-corrosive, stainless steel in the R-101, using fewer but stronger members to get adequate strength without addition of weight. A Detroit experiment of a ship with a shell-thin metal cover in place of fabric is another example of the search for improvement.

And some measure of that progress as between 1915 and 1930 may be found in an increase in speed from 45 m. p. h. to 80, in cruising range from a few hundred miles to 10,000, in ceiling from 2,000 to a height in the case of hydrogen ships, of 24,000, and in strength and carrying capacity in even greater ratios.

There are still other improvements being built into the two great American airships which will be referred to in the chapter describing those vessels.

CHAPTER XI

The New Navy Airships

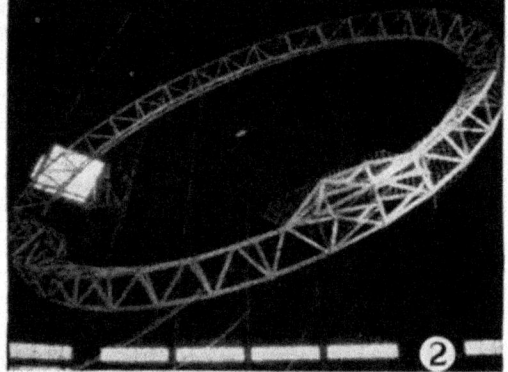

Raising the first ring girder in construction of the U. S. S. Akron. 1. Shows girder on floor before raising. 2. The ring being raised by electrical cranes to a vertical position.

THE new American Navy ships, "The Akron" and ZRS-5, authorized by Congress, the first of which is now under construction at Akron, were to be not only the largest but the fastest and strongest airships ever built.

What would the airship designer, familiar with past practice, do to improve the 1930 airship? This was the problem facing Dr. Arnstein, his staff and the Navy engineers.

What improvements could be added besides increasing size, strength, and lift? The designers found several, each marking a significant forward step.

Every Zeppelin ship has a metal keel or backbone, its major reinforcement against vertical thrusts of the wind which might be of uneven force along a vessel nearly three city blocks long.

However, "The Akron" has three such keels instead of one. Some idea of the increase in strength may be realized by the simple illustration of lashing three lead pencils together and trying to break them, as compared to breaking a single pencil.

The keel of an airship is built large enough to contain a corridor or catwalk running from one end of the ship to the other, giving accessibility throughout the ship, offering space alongside for fuel, ballast, passenger or crew quarters, baggage and mail compartments.

The new American ships retain this corridor feature, but by placing one of these corridors or backbones at the top of the ship and the other two at 45 degrees from the bottom, the accessibility to service facilities and to maintenance are more than tripled.

Since a gas leak, if one occurs, can be repaired in flight, the value of constant inspection of every part of the ship is a safety factor of great importance. No Zeppelin ship has ever been so completely accessible to inspection as these will be.

For example, any gas expands and contracts due to changes in temperature, altitude and barometric pressure so that valves are provided on all lighter-than-air craft, in case expansion should reach the maximum capacity of the bag—when the surplus is released through the valves immediately and automatically without bringing any strain on the ship.

These automatic valves have been placed at the bottom of the gas cell in the past, with a smaller number of additional cells at the top, manually operated from the control car.

In "The Akron" all the valves, automatic and manual, are placed at the top where, since the gas is lighter than air and flows upward, immediate release can be had. The valves are installed along the top

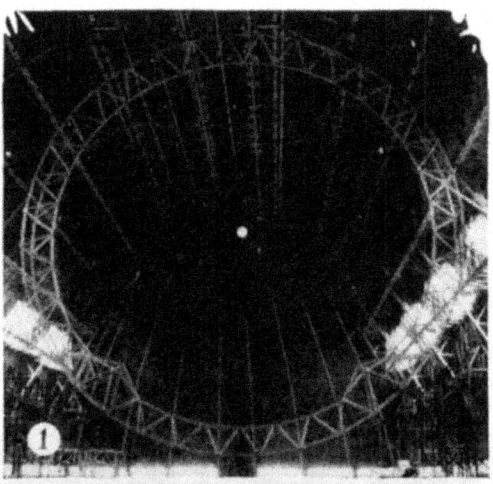

1. First ring girder or main frame in position which it occupies in completed ship. 2. As other rings are added, the form of the ship rapidly develops.

keel or corridor so that the commander may be sure at all times they are in perfect working order.

The Goodyear-Zeppelin Corporation evolved a new type of main ring or frame. These are of triangular cross section, each being built inherently strong, without the great net-work of wiring used in previous types, a spider web of wire netting being used between gas cells merely to hold them in place and designed so that they cannot catch in the cell or chafe against it.

Strengthening of the ship permitted another improvement. Up to 1924 most control cars and all integrally into the hull of the ship.

"The Akron" takes the next step forward and for the first time in history, places the engines inside the ship. The cutting down of resistance is obvious. Also the cramped quarters of power cars which were made as small as possible to cut down air resistance, give way in the new ships to comfortable engine rooms.

The use of helium permits this to be done with entire safety and the stronger framework absorbs the load as a part of the ship.

Another interesting improvement. With hydrogen ships, past

Testing one of the gas cells which will provide lifting power for the U. S. S. Akron. The gas cell occupies a bay or the space between two girders. The racing balloon at the right was used as an auxiliary storage tank for the helium gas in the test.

power cars were suspended on outriggers outside the body of the ship. Early ships usually had one engine mounted in the rear of the control car. And since all ships were hydrogen-inflated, it was necessary to get complete ventilation, to prevent the possibility of sparks from the motors coming in contact with the lifting gas.

In the Los Angeles, however, the engine was omitted from the control car and given a separate gondola, and the control car was built practice had been to release lifting gas from time to time to compensate for the steadily decreasing weight of the ship due to the consumption of gasoline fuel.

It will be recalled that in the Graf Zeppelin the constructors tried to get away from this hydrogen loss by using Blau gas as fuel. Since the Blau gas had approximately the weight of air, its consumption as fuel didn't change the ship's weight.

Three years earlier, American

engineers got around the difficulty another way, being especially impelled to do so because the helium gas was more expensive than hydrogen, was a natural resource and could not be reproduced at will. They devised exhaust condensers and installed them on the engines.

Ballast-recovery devices, as they were called, condensed the water vapor in the exhaust gases into water which was actually a trifle heavier than the gasoline burned. This not only conserved the helium, but had an operating advantage in that the Los Angeles could start on a journey with a minimum quantity of ballast, building up its supply as it went along, thus increasing its cruising radius by permitting it to start off with more fuel in place of the heavier ballast load formerly carried.

The condensers, however, added somewhat to the parasitical resistance, and since the motors of "The Akron" were to be inside anyhow, a condenser system was devised composed of small ribbed fins along the side of the ship, something like the louvres in the hood of an automobile, getting a maximum cooling result with minimum resistance.

The fifth improvement brought out in "The Akron" is the device of swiveling propellers. These can be swung in a 90-degree arc, and since the engines are reversible, give the ship vertical thrust, down or up.

The swiveling feature will be valuable in maneuvering the ship, especially in landings and take-offs. Pointed downward to exert a vertical thrust this will enable a ship to take off "heavy," carrying additional fuel and so increasing the cruising radius. They can be used also to drive the ship downward if it comes in for landing "light," due to atmospheric conditions or other causes.

The last and perhaps most interesting of the improvements in "The Akron" is the airplane compartment, where space for five airplanes is provided in the hull. This storage "hangar" is 75x60 feet in size, and is located about one-third of the ship's length from the nose. Planes may be released through a T-shaped opening in the ship's bottom by a trapeze arrangement, while the ship is in flight. They may be picked up again on the trapeze, and hauled into the compartment by a winch. Such a provision increases the scouting value of a military airship and aids her in warding off attack, while in case of a commercial ship would permit passengers to embark or disembark en route without stopping the ship itself. Or a tardy passenger on a transatlantic flight might take a high-speed plane and overtake the airship at sea.

The table on the next page shows the principal characteristics of the several ships. One interesting point is the slenderness ratio, that is, the ratio of length to diameter. Mass production requirements of war times favored a lead pencil shape with the ring girders all uniform in size except at the two ends. That this involved some sacrifice of

Intricate construction of ship's framework clearly pictured. There are 6,500,000 rivets in the entire framework construction—by coincidence, a rivet for every cubic foot of the ship's capacity.

Applying outer covering to completed framework of U. S. S. Akron. Work of covering was begun at nose. Photograph taken in February, 1931.

efficiency was realized by the constructors, but it was not until after the war that they were free to build the ships in the shorter, more rounded shape, tapering to both ends.

The Shenandoah had a ratio of 8.7, was eight times as long as it was thick, whereas the Los Angeles has a ratio of 7.2. Due to the size and shape of its largest hangar, the Graf Zeppelin was not able to reach the ideal proportions. It is only nine feet shorter than the American "The Akron" which has almost twice the volume; the American ship will be a third greater in diameter. The new German ship LZ-128, now under construction, will use a slenderness ratio representing present engineering thought on this subject.

The ratio of 6.0 adopted for "The Akron" was arrived at after exhaustive wind tunnel tests and the weighing of factors of strength, controllability, and the like involved. The comparison of four typical Zeppelins follows:

	Los Angeles	Graf Zeppelin	R-100	"The Akron"
Nominal Gas Volume, cubic feet	2,470,000	3,700,000	5,000,000	6,500,000
Length Over-all, feet	658.3	776	709	785
Maximum Diameter, feet	90.7	100	131	132.9
Height Over-all, feet	104.4	113	138	146.5
Slenderness Ratio	7.2	7.7	5.3	6.0
Gross Lift, pounds	153,000	258,000	335,000	403,000
Useful Lift, pounds	60,000	100,000	117,000	182,000
Number of Engines	5	5	6	8
Total Horsepower	2,000	2,750	4,250	4,480
Maximum Speed, M.P.H.	73	80	80	84
Range without Refueling at Cruising Speed—Land Miles	4,000	6,125	4,200	10,580

CHAPTER XII

How the Akron Was Built

SINCE the Akron is but the second rigid airship to be built in the United States, most people have little idea of how one goes about it to build one. So here is the story briefly of its construction.

Since the work starts with the metal skeleton, carloads of sheet duralumin began rumbling into Akron from the mills of the Aluminum Company of America at Pittsburgh, long before the construction dock was completed.

In the airship shop nearby, strips of "dural," six to nine inches wide, were presently being fed to great presses which turned up the edges, punched lightening holes in, turned up their edges. There were large holes, small ones, middle size holes till it seemed that only a shell remained. These lightening holes, which were shortly to give the ship structure the appearance of a fret work of Irish lace, cut the dead weight in two, by cutting out half of the metal, and yet when small flanges had been machine-turned around each hole, left the perforated strip actually stronger than if it had remained one solid piece.

These channel sections, as they are called, were then ready to be riveted together, to form a four-sided box girder section.

Airships must fly in all weathers and one of the useful properties of duralumin is that it is highly resistant to corrosion, that is to say, rust. However, it was desired to make the Akron still more indifferent to weather and give it longer life than any former airship. So before the channel sections were assembled into girders every piece of duralumin was anodized and then varnished. The Akron was the first airship to be so treated. Even the 6,500,000 rivets put into the ship were anodized. The rivets were then heat treated and inserted in a semi-soft condition, resuming their natural hardness after 24 to 48 hours.

Next came the assembly of girders to form giant rings, the largest of these 135 feet in diameter—that is, if set upright like a huge hoop they would be as high as a 14 story building. The rings were not to be round but polygons with 36 sides (though the smaller rings toward the tail would have only 24 sides). Each main ring (a main ring in navy parlance is a frame) is really a series of three rings, two on the outside, one on the inside, forming a great circular triangle, braced zigzag fashion with sturdy duralumin struts.

It was this type of construction that made the main rings or frames inherently strong, able to stand alone without reinforcement.

Past practice in building had been to erect first a great cradle or steel scaffold into which the ship would be built. Since the main frames of the Akron were inherently strong, they were built flat on the floor and when completed were hoisted into the upright position they were to have in the ship.

The raising of the frames made an interesting picture. First the lighter intermediate rings were lashed to the main ring. Then ropes were attached at many points around the circle to distribute the load and these ropes attached to a cable, reaching to a pulley in the roof, and from there to a hoist below. Other lines were attached to guide the ring, whistles were blown, messages sent aloft and over the building by portable telephone, then the cable began to wind up on the drum, and the giant ring, weighing some two tons, suspended from a huge spider web of

1. Vivid photograph taken from catwalk at top of dock, showing crowd of 30,000 assembled around the master ring to witness ring laying ceremony marking beginning of construction of U. S. S. Akron, November, 1929, in Goodyear-Zeppelin dock at Akron. 2. Admiral W. A. Moffett, Chief of the Naval Bureau of Aeronautics, addresses the nation via radio on the significance of the ring laying. 3. Admiral Moffett drives a golden rivet into main section of master ring. P. W. Litchfield, president of Goodyear-Zeppelin Corp., at the right. 4. Dr. Karl Arnstein, vice president of Goodyear-Zeppelin and designer of U. S. S. Akron, tells about future of lighter-than-air. 5. President P. W. Litchfield, father of the lighter-than-air development in America, addresses radio audience at ring laying. 6. Another view of the crowds witnessing the ceremony. The background is one of the giant 600-ton doors of the dock.

ropes, moved easily aloft, was carried over and set in place without the slightest jar.

Once two main frames had been set up, the intermediate frames were spaced into position between, and the longitudinal girders were riveted into place like mighty staves of a giant's barrel.

In similar fashion the assembly proceeded, three or four frames being under construction simultaneously, were hoisted aloft as fast as completed. Nose and tail, cone shaped, were assembled on the floor, picked up dexterously, carried aloft.

After the first frames were in place, a test gas cell was built, inserted into the structure, filled with helium and floated into position—to make sure that it would fit snugly between the bulwarks of the duralumin framework and the steel network of wires.

This test cell contained 900,000 cubic feet of helium gas. It alone was larger than the Italian Norge that flew over the North Pole, was almost half as big as the U. S. S. Los Angeles. The test completed, the helium was pumped back to wait until needed again.

Simultaneously with the construction of the ship, work on the eight 560 h. p. engines got under way at Friedrichshafen, Germany. The Maybach company, a Zeppelin subsidiary, which furnished the engines for the Los Angeles and the Graf Zeppelin, presently shipped the new engines to Akron where reinforced duralumin engine mounts had been built into the ship.

The Allison Engineering Company of Indianapolis worked out the problem of transmission and gearing, a challenging problem since the Akron utilized a remote drive principle. The propellers, instead of being mounted immediately to the engine, were to be set 18 feet away, projecting outside of the ship on outrigger mountings of chrome molybdenum steel. Moreover, a socket joint had to be

Covering U. S. S. Akron with outer fabric. Picture taken in May, 1931.

evolved so that the propellers could be tilted through a 90-degree arc. The Zeppelin Company at Friedrichshafen was also asked to design a transmission system, and this as well as the American one tested out satisfactorily, so that one of the German transmissions was installed on the Akron along with the Allison ones.

Type tests were required for the new transmission; so a section of the ship was built in full scale alongside the airship factory, engine and transmission were mounted, and there hour after hour and day after day, the power plant was tested out—at full speed, cruising, idling, ahead and astern and with the propeller set for vertical thrust, until all were satisfied that the power plant was in order and ready for installation on shipboard.

The huge fins, 120 feet long, 35 feet wide at the widest point, deep enough for men to walk about erect inside, made up the last part of the ship structure. Two of them were mounted in a vertical position and two in the horizontal to make the vessel aerodynamically stable, with a movable section 15

Side view of U. S. S. Akron showing application of outer covering, May, 1931.

feet long, called elevators in one case, rudders in the other, to give it maneuverability up and down or left and right. The leading edges of the fins, great shells of burnished duralumin nearly four feet wide, were among the few pieces of solid metal, outside of the nose cone and tail cap, in the ship's structure.

Control lines, steel cables, tremendously strong, were installed, reaching from the control room back to the control surfaces 600 feet away, running smoothly on some 2,000 sheaves, or pulleys, so that a simple turn of the steering wheel or elevator wheel would be reflected instantly in the distant rudders or elevators and so drive the ship on a given course and inclination.

Of the 160 odd airships built in the world none has ever had a major failure of the control lines, except in two cases during the war when the ships were steered from emergency controls in the tail. However, all Zeppelin type ships have had such emergency control systems. In the Akron duplicate steering wheel and elevator wheels, winches and cables were built into the lower vertical fin—which was large enough to provide a comfortable workroom for the helmsmen and elevator men if the emergency should ever arise.

The control room was proportionately one of the smallest ever built for a Zeppelin type ship, since it was to house only the control and navigation facilities; quarters, officers, radio room and all else being placed elsewhere. Thus the captain of the Akron, standing at the bridge, can look over his shoulder and see the bumper under the lower fin 600 feet away, can visually check the trim of his ship at take-offs and landings.

While the metal structure was being assembled, the balloon room at Goodyear, which had built hundreds of balloons and small airships, was at work building an outer cover seven acres in size, and the 12 gas cells of rubberized and gelatine latex fabric.

The outer cover, very light, very strong—having a 60 pound per inch breaking strength (which when the cover was doped would increase to 84 pounds)—was made up in sections which would just fit the space from one girder to the next. They put in hundreds of eyelets of tiny feather-heavy dural rings, machine stitched, along the four edges. A class was organized to teach the workmen how to lace the cover to the framework, and how to dope it afterward. Three weeks practice on the ground was stipulated before the men were judged ready to go aloft to "dress" the ship.

Then working from curious ladders, 85 feet high (which were mounted on trucks so that they would not have to lean against anything), the men went aloft, carrying the sections of outer cover. Other men worked from platforms suspended from the roof, sometimes from a set of platforms, ranged in tiers one above the other, and quickly dubbed "pie racks."

The cover sections were laced taut, left to stand a day, tightened, left a day, tightened again.

The doping, which waterproofed the cover and further shrunk it till it was taut as a drum head, was done after the fabric had been placed in position and had a chance to "set." The interstices between girders are smaller on the Akron than in previous practice, making for a smooth cover with low resistance.

The first coat of dope was painted on by hand, then with a day in between to dry, three more were sprayed on, the last two coats being mixed with aluminum pigment, which reflected the sun's rays, rather than absorbed them, protected the dope from weathering, gave the ship its familiar silvery hue, made it semi-metallic.

As the ship neared completion, visitors noticed a network of girders amidships. This proved to be the hangar for airplanes, with a monorail on which the planes were to ride into position aboard ship, a trapeze for the plane to hook on, and a winch for hoisting them aboard or lowering them to flight position.

The "flying hangar" extends across the lower segment of the airship, the gas cell over it being just a little shorter, to make room for it.

The decks of quarters were built of stiff light balsa wood with a film-thin surface of cold rolled aluminum.

Gun mounts for the machine guns, strong enough to take the recoil of powerful armament, were built into the ship structure at designated strategic points, though the actual arming of the vessel was to wait until it was commissioned into the naval service.

More than 800 business houses supplied material or equipment for the Akron and so, as the ship construction progressed, firms all over the country, were shipping in supplies, ranging from great pneumatic presses to tiny grommets. There were many new problems presented. Weight was always a factor. And manufacturers and research men took this as a challenge to their ingenuity and resourcefulness and evolved here and there, in aluminum and chrome steel and molybdenum and stainless steel results that may be widely applied elsewhere.

The list of suppliers starts properly with the Aluminum Co. of America, since the main structure of the ship is made of duralumin,

Doors of giant dock open showing construction of U. S. S. Akron.

and this company was able to develop a special cold rolled dural that more than met the exacting specifications set up. The American Steel & Wire Co., produced a hard steel wire, highly resistant to corrosion (since the Akron is to be a salt-water vessel) and supplied some thirty miles of it for girder bracing and for the spider web bulwarks, separating the gas cells.

Westinghouse made up the most powerful radio set ever installed in aircraft, furnished devices for communication and electrical equipment; Upson and Walton, Cleveland ship chandlers' furnished 30 miles of hempen rope used in rigging the ship and for the handling lines, made up special rope in one instance from flax grown in Scotland; the Wellman Engineering Company, who had built the "orange peel" doors, now built the mobile mast; the Cleveland Pneumatic Tool Co., worked out resiliency devices to take up the slack as the gas cells contracted and expanded; an Illinois firm, the Independent Pneumatic Tool Co., built tiny electric drills, weighing two pounds and 13 ounces, including the motors; SKF and Fafnir made up hundreds of tiny bearings to make smooth mechanisms all over the ship.

The Otis Elevator Co., built the curious elevators, like inverted funicular railways that climb smoothly up the side wall and around under the curving roof of the airship dock to the top catwalks, the first of its kind ever built; the American Magirus Co., made the strange ladders that caught every visitor's eye; the A. O. Smith Co., of Milwaukee, devised the great helium containers; the Great Lakes Aircraft Corp. at Cleveland, manufacturers of airplanes, helped out many times on special jobs that would otherwise have involved expensive special equipment; the American Bridge Co., tackled the great task of erecting the structure of the building itself with its huge center arches, weighing many tons.

Many cotton mills worked at the problem of light, tough fabrics for outer covers and gas cells; The Waltham Co., watchmakers, made delicate parts for tiny instruments to test the stresses in reenforcing wires; as dural rivets are not driven into place but squeezed in after heat-treating and while still semi-soft, curiously shaped squeezers, to get into the network of girders — S-shaped, G-shaped, "dog leg" "lobster claws," so the men dubbed them—were made by the Whitney Metal Co., at Rockford, Ind.; the Pittsburgh Plate Glass Co., made the glass windows that must face the air impacts at the front of the control car, the side windows being made of acetate celluloid; the Kellogg Switchboard Co., worked out an ultra light telephone system, for the ship; the Tappan Stove Co., of Mansfield, built an aluminum cook stove (Propane-heated) that would serve 50 men, yet which weighed but 110 pounds; the Serry Machine Co., at Kent, Ohio, developed new processes of working stainless steel; even the makers of wash room equipment; the Imperial Brass Co., turned out special stuff, light, durable.

And so the list might be extended, through General Electric, DuPont, Sherwin-Williams, Roeblings, American Rolling Mills, Revere Brass, the great steel companies, through many pages. Each had a part in building the greatest airship. All took a deep interest in the job. Many of them made real contributions.

Scheme of triangular main ring structure of the 6,500,000-cubic-foot airships ordered by the U. S. Navy. Each ring gives access by Members of the crew to all longitudinal corridors and all parts of the hull.

CHAPTER XIII

Safety of Rigid Airship

SAFETY in rigid airship operation begins with the construction of the ship itself.

Remember that a Zeppelin ship starts with a complete metal framework which consists of a series of huge rings of varying diameter and these connected by longitudinal girders, extending from nose to tail. And that the gas is carried in 11 to 20 cells placed in bays between the ring girders instead of being contained in a single bag as in the case of the non-rigids. This system, inherent in the Zeppelin type, gives the airship a protection similar to the bulkheads of a ship. If one or two gas cells should be wrecked and lose all their gas, the remaining gas cells would still have buoyancy enough to keep the ships in the air.

Essential in the Zeppelin type airship is the principle of various parts reinforcing and, if necessary, replacing the function of others.

I quote again from Dr. Karl Arnstein in his paper, "The Development of Large Commercial Airships," given before the Aeronautic Section of the American Society of Mechanical Engineers, in 1928. He says:

"In the single-cover system, most typically represented in the non-rigid type of envelope, this cover must hold the lifting gas, take all stresses of static or dynamic origin, and serve as a cover against rain, hail, or snow. Thus damage to the single cover impairs it in respect to all of the three functions it serves.

"In the rigid airship three units

are provided, one for each of these purposes. The gas cells serve for the retention of the gas; a complete metal framework surrounding these gas cells takes all stresses, securing maximum strength with minimum weight, and the whole is enclosed by a taut doped and metallized fabric cover for protection again the elements, which reflects heat and offers a smooth flying surface. A network surrounding the gas cells protects them against expansion, while the air space between outer cover and gas cells serves as valuable ventilating space.

"This arrangement of dividing the functions has the advantage that one structural part may replace or assist another. This means, for instance, that the outer cover, if properly applied and maintained, will act as a valuable stress-bearing unit, lowering the stresses in the metal structure and taking shear forces even with the structure intact. Or in case of the destruction of a part of the metal framework, the fabric at this point conveys shear forces from one intact section to the other. These features make the rigid airship a very rugged and coherent structure."

Speaking of this power plant he says: "The large airship has so many motor units that the failure of even two of them does not endanger the ship's safety or even reduce the speed to a serious degree."

There are five motors separately housed in the Los Angeles and the Graf Zeppelin. "The Akron" has eight.

Moreover the modern airship, while having available the accumulated experience of 30 years of airship building and flying, has stimulated extensive research into the most exact measurement of the stresses that will be encountered by any portion of the ship and has developed its own science of calculating these and of gauging the strength of the materials which encounter such stresses.

Setting up the premise that the modern airship will be well built, let us examine the various weather phenomena that it may encounter in flight to see what the effect of each of these is.

I summarize the comments of Capt. Ernst Lehmann, first officer of the Graf Zeppelin, in a paper also given before the American Society of Mechanical Engineers in 1926 on "The Safety of Zeppelins."

Rain—The cover of the airship is doped to resist water. Rain is only an inconvenience.

Snow—On account of the speed of the ship the snow blows off in flight, except wet snow, in which case the captain will slightly change the altitude of the ship and get into drier air. If the snow falls on the ship at the mast it may be necessary to take off and make a short flight to give the wind a chance to clear it off.

Hail—Even the largest hailstones do no damage to the airship, as the outer cover has the same strength as metal of the same thickness and is, of course, more resilient.

Girls at work in Goodyear-Zeppelin balloon room splicing fabric ship covering.

Cold—The lift of the ship is better in cold weather than in warm and permits extra provisions being made for the comfort of the crew if necessary.

Heat—this has some effect on the buoyancy since the air is lighter and more rarefied but offers no special operating difficulties. Airships have flown successfully in the tropics.

Wind—The effect of wind on the airship is not entirely understood because of the comparison of its effect on anchored objects like trees or houses or those moving slowly like ocean vessels.

The airship, however, is moving with the air currents. If a ship were to fly in a 60-mile gale with all its engines shut off like a free balloon, the passengers would be conscious of no sense of motion at all. If they stuck a hand out of the window there would be no rush of air past it.

The airship during such a gale is not subject to anything like the stresses tugging at a house which cannot move, or a ship at sea the response of which to the wind's movements is impeded by the water.

If the wind is moving in the same direction as the ship it merely increases its speed to that extent. If flying against the wind its forward speed is retarded. An 80-mile-an-hour airship bucking a 30-mile wind would be actually making only 50 m. p. h.

The airship skipper figures shrewdly to take advantage of winds and hunts for storms rather than avoids them.

Storms generally move across the country in regular cycles at comparatively low forward speeds and with a turning movement, counter-clockwise, in the northern hemisphere, that is in the opposite direction of the hands of a clock.

The airship commander, wishing to utilize the storm, maneuvers to get the wind at his back so it will carry him in the direction sought.

One of the eight swiveling propellers that can be swung in a ninety degree arc and since the motors are reversible give the ship 180 degrees in directional or altitudinal control. The picture shows Lt. T. G. W. Settle, U. S. N. and Dr. Karl Arnstein inspecting a test installation.

He actually utilizes the storm to save fuel.

Operation of airships over land, however, has one element which exists only in a smaller degree over the ocean—that is local storms, gusts and turbulences which result from the uneven character of the ground, hills and valleys, and from the unequal heating of the earth's surface.

When the air is warmer at one point than at another the cold air rushes in forcing the warm air up. An unequal heating over a considerable area brings about uneven winds, thunderstorms and the great fronts of rising air known as line squalls.

An airship captain meeting a line squall puts his ship in equilibrium, flying it as close to the ground as practicable. If the front is too wide for him to fly around he will watch for an opening where the storm is not fully developed and break through.

The presence of such openings may be recognized by the cloud formation by day and the absence of lightning by night.

Lightning—The metal framework of the rigid airship forms a "Faraday Cage" where lightning if it hits the airship is distributed and escapes harmlessly through the engine exhaust and at other safe points. Rigid airships have been struck by lightning many times, even those filled with hydrogen. If a commander keeps his ship below the "pressure height" so that no hydrogen is being forced out through the valves he can get through without difficulty.

With helium, of course, the lightning danger doesn't exist.

Fog—The airship has an advantage here over the airplane. Whereas a landing in the fog is highly hazardous to an airplane, the airship can simply throttle down its speed and descend vertically, feeling its way to the mooring mast or the hangar. Fogs are usually not accompanied by high winds so this maneuver is not difficult.

Tornado—This is the one phenomenon about which complete meteorological data does not exist, but a tornado is only a twister or a whirling movement, on a larger scale. Since the area of the tornado is usually quite limited, the airship should have no difficulty in avoiding them.

Typhoons—The Graf Zeppelin encountered these twice near Japan, on the world flight, but found them only stronger storm areas. Instead of running away from them, Dr. Eckener, on both occasions, maneuvered his ship into the tail of the storm, put the tyhpoon to work for him, expediting his arrival at Japan and his departure from the islands, with appreciable savings in fuel consumption and time, making the run to Los Angeles across the Pacific Ocean in three days.

—Photo No. 2 Courtesy Hamburg-American Line.

When Dr. Eckener returned from U. S. to Germany on the S. S. New York of the Hamburg-American Line, the Graf Zeppelin with a party of his friends and relatives aboard flew out to sea to the steamship as it approached Hamburg. Although the New York appears dwarfed, the steamship is actually but 142 feet shorter than the dirigible.

Helium repurifying machine at Akron. Gas can be removed from the non-rigid type of airship or from gas cells of rigid ships and passed through this machine for repurification and further use.

CHAPTER XIV

Helium and Duralumin

ONE of the most interesting of the natural gases and one highly important to aeronautics is helium.

Helium is next to hydrogen in density, being about one-seventh the weight of air. Stated another way, 1,000 cubic feet of hydrogen at 32° temperature, at sea level, will lift 75.1 pounds while the same volume of helium will lift 69.6 pounds.

As one consequence, a helium ship has to be built larger than one inflated with hydrogen in order to get the same lift. And since a helium ship starts a given flight with its gas cells only partly inflated, averaging 85 to 90 per cent, so that as the gas expands with changes in temperature and altitude, the cells are merely filled completely and don't overflow,—a 6,500,000-cubic-foot helium ship would have approximately the same useful lift as a 5,000,000-cubic-foot hydrogen.

Against this slight disadvantage in lift, however, is the supreme advantage that helium is non-inflammable—it not only does not burn, but will put out a fire.

It is the use of helium in the new American ships that has permitted the engines to be installed inside the ship itself, instead of in cars suspended outside on outriggers.

And the special significance of helium to the United States is the fact that helium is a natural resource, and that America has practically a monopoly of this gas. Also the further fact that there is apparently ample supply in sight to cover requirements for many years ahead.

The story of the discovery of helium is interesting. In 1868, Jannsen, French astronomer, noted a line, bright yellow, in the spectrum of the sun during an eclipse, one not previously recorded.

Franklin and Lockyer, British scientists, in 1868 showed that the line was caused by a new element not known on earth. They called it helium, from "helios," the Greek word for sun. It was found in 1907, and later, in natural gas in certain parts of the country—Kansas, Texas, Utah, Wyoming. A method was worked out during the war for separating helium from the natural gas in large quantities, and a government plant was erected at Fort Worth, Texas, the remaining natural gas being returned to the city mains.

In 1929, due to the field becoming depleted, the plant was moved to Amarillo, Texas, where the government had acquired gas rights. It is estimated that there are ten billion cubic feet of helium in sight in the United States, enough for all airship uses for many years to come.

Cost of helium production has been brought down from $450 per thousand cubic feet to $15. It is still about twice as expensive as hydrogen in first cost, but, since helium can be repurified and used over and over, its actual cost is less than hydrogen. It is impracticable to try to purify hydrogen.

The Army, Navy and Goodyear Zeppelin all maintain their own purification plants. Helium losses due to diffusion and other causes run from five to eight per cent per month in the Goodyear fleet.

In addition to the government plant there are private plants at Dexter, Kansas, and Thatcher, Colorado. In the Colorado field gas has been found with a helium content as high as eight per cent.

However, even if the cost of operating helium ships were much greater than it is, the advantage of maximum safety would be worth the difference.

Since 1922 all government airships and the Goodyear fleet of non-rigids have been helium-inflated.

Quantities of helium had been assembled at New Orleans, awaiting shipment to France, when the armistice was signed.

The Goodyear-Zeppelin Corporation has installed 96 unusual helium storage tanks underground alongside the dock at Akron where a million feet of helium is compressed and stored under 750 pounds pressure. The tanks, 96 in number, are 80 feet long, two feet in diameter. The balance of the gas needed for The Akron is stored in the conventional gas tanks, four feet long, a foot in diameter, which are stacked in tiers on the ground close at hand.

Placing of underground storage tanks at Goodyear-Zeppelin Corporation airship dock in Akron, which have a capacity of more than a million cubic feet of helium.

Duralumin

Highly important in the pioneering days of the airship was the development of the metal duralumin.

Duralumin, an alloy of aluminum which combines the lightness of aluminum with the strength of steel, makes practicable the construction of the huge framework of the big ships.

Duralumin was first produced in Duren, Germany, after a process developed by Dr. A. Wilm. It is one of a number of alloys known as the "hard aluminums." Duralumin is about 94 per cent aluminum with small amounts of copper, manganese and magnesium. The magnesium combines with silicon which is present in the aluminum as an impurity and gives duralumin some of its useful characteristics. Duralumin is about one-third the weight of steel.

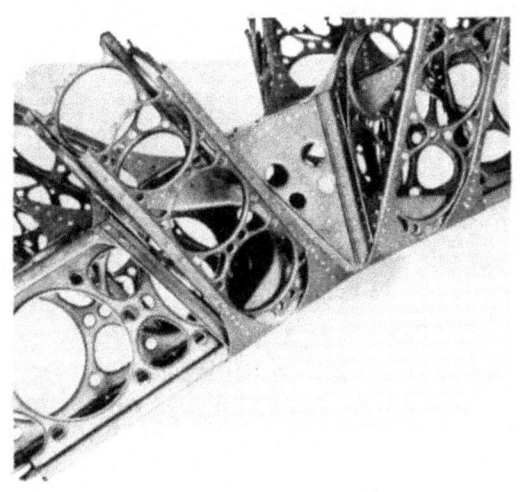

Detail of large airship main ring girders and struts at point of junction.

CHAPTER XV
Military Uses of the Airship

ONE way of appraising the military value of the airship is to see just what has been accomplished by it in actual warfare, add to that the new developments made since the war, subtract the improvements in methods of defense against airships and in methods of attacking airships.

The data as to actual use in the past is not, of course, complete enough to permit final judgments to be arrived at. Airships have been used in but one war, and principally by one nation in that war. However, many of the actual facts are available for analysis.

The layman is apt to think of Zeppelin ships in terms of the London raids. The effect of these was largely discounted at the time, but it is generally conceded since that they had rather substantial results.

They handicapped and delayed the manufacture and shipment of war material, since lights were turned off and traffic stopped over a considerable area during the 24-48-hour period of a raid. Also they served to hold in England for home defense, thousands of soldiers and guns which otherwise might have turned the tide of battle in France.

However, these raids, while spectacular, made up only about 10 per cent of the actual activities of the airships. Their real use was in scouting and reconnaissance with the fleet where on more than one occasion a Zeppelin scout saved a German fleet from being cut off by the British. The most significant indication of their usefulness to the Navy comes from men who fought against them. I quote from a war time British report:

"From the results already given of instances, it will be seen how

Navy ship Los Angeles circling Akron, Ohio.

justified is the confidence felt by the German Navy in its airships when used in their proper sphere as the eyes of the fleet. It is no small achievement for their Zeppelins to have saved the high seas fleet at the battle of Jutland, to have saved their cruiser squadron on the Yarmouth raid, and to have been instrumental in sinking the Nottingham and Falmouth. Had the positions been reversed in the Jutland battle, and had we had rigids to enable us to locate and annihilate the German High Seas Fleet, can anyone deny the far-reaching effects it would have had in ending the war?"

Great Britain's real interest in rigid airships began during the war, when an active construction program was started.

However, Britain's most spectacular use of lighter-than-air came with the smaller non-rigids or blimps.

The activities of British, French and American non-rigids were little heard of during the World War, being obscured by greater events, and the censorship. However, British non-rigids alone, according to official reports, covered 2,245,000 miles during the war, almost as many as the great Zeppelins. Including all training and experimental flying, in addition to all deaths resulting from enemy action, only 48 lives were lost.

Let us quote from Rear Admiral W. A. Moffett, Chief of the Bureau of Aeronautics, appearing before the House Committee on Naval Affairs:

"During the World War, as far as we know, no convoy was ever attacked by a submarine when guarded by an airship. During the 17 months prior to the Armistice, British airships sighted 49 submarines and successfully attacked 27 of them; they convoyed 2,000 surface vessels and carried out over 9,000 anti-submarine patrols; and from January 1 to November 11, 1918, there were only nine days in which these airships could not fly because of bad weather.

"From the war diaries of submarine commanders, it can be seen that the fear of the airship entertained by the submarine applied to both British and German services. That this fear was justified is amply proved by a number of cases such as that of the British E-18 which was sighted and bombed by a Zeppelin while lying in 70 feet of water."

The war brought many improvements in performance on the part of the Zeppelins. Speed increased to 70 m. p. h.; the altitude to which ships could mount, to 25,000 feet and higher; the carrying capacity was more than doubled.

Every new instrument of warfare brings a new method of defense. In the case of the airship this was largely anti-aircraft guns and fast airplanes shooting inflammable bullets.

Anti-aircraft guns are now mounted on ships, and airplanes

may go to sea and be catapulted from the decks of battleships or take off from floating carriers like the Saratoga and the Lexington.

How will the airship meet these new dangers?

The most important airship improvement since the war is helium gas. All of the airship's work during the World War, meeting the attacks of ocean ships, land batteries and airplanes, was done with hydrogen gas which is inflammable, and under certain conditions explosive.

Helium will not burn.

The loss of a gas cell in a rigid ship will not send it to the ground but merely reduces its buoyancy. Local repairs in the case of bullet holes can be made quickly and easily during flights. The airship can keep out of the range of anti-aircraft guns whether mounted on shipboard or on coasts. It can disregard three of the dangers which the fleet faces—those of ships, of torpedoes, or submarines.

Against airplanes the airship would carry machine guns, and even light artillery mounted on top, in the nose, in the tail, in the engine cars and control car. It can climb to upper altitudes faster than

1. Another view of a Navy kite or observation balloon. 2. Interior of U. S. Naval hangar at Lakehurst, N. J. The several ships include the Los Angeles, non-rigid training ships and the Graf Zeppelin.

the airplane and if pursued by airplanes, would be returning their fire from a superior altitude, and with a more stable base for its gun carriages.

Ships of "The Akron" type will have a tremendous advantage in that they will carry floating hangars inside the hull with room for five fighting airplanes, which may be released or taken aboard at will during flight, and available for attack or defense.

Naval experts have estimated that a fleet of ten airships could patrol the entire Atlantic ocean preventing any concentrated movement against the American coast, being unobserved and unchallenged.

The naval airship will not make any other type of craft obsolete, but it will relieve surface craft of a great deal of the cruising work thus permitting a greater concentration of men, money and metal in fighting units.

It will supplement the ocean-going airplane carrier of the Lexington and Saratoga type, on account of its greater speed and will aid in the quick concentration of airplanes as needed.

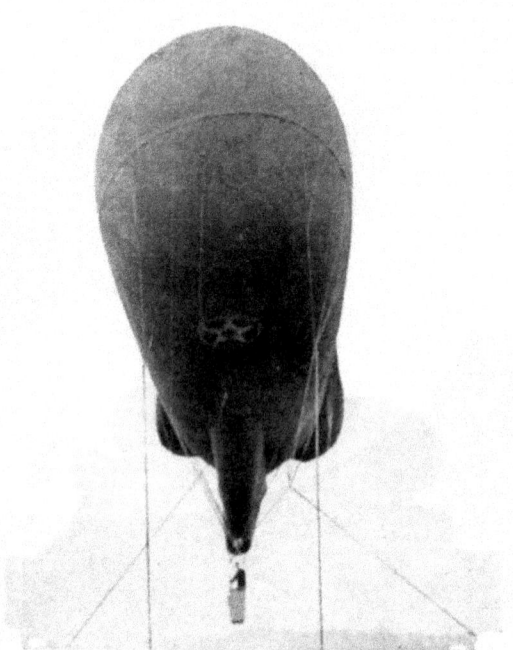

Captive observation or "sausage" balloon used for military purposes. Observer is in basket.

CHAPTER XVI

Airship Handling

Commander C. E. Rosendahl captain of U. S. S. Akron.

THE landing of an airship is an impressive sight. With radioed news of the ship's approach the landing crew, some three or four hundred men, take their places, the main body in a great V-formation, small groups forming a lane fronting the open end of the V. The lane faces into the wind, since the ship will land to the wind.

Presently the Zeppelin emerges from the haze, draws majestically closer, nosing gradually downward. Humming engines grow louder, then are checked as the ship nears the landing space. Two are set in astern to check the momentum. A small hatchway opens, forward, and a bundle drops, opens in falling, is recognized as the landing line. The men catch it, attach spider web lines, so that 20 may hold. Other lines drop now. The ship loses momentum as the motors ease off. The men pull steadily on the lines, a group moves forward to the control car, catches the handling rails. A moment later contact is made. The ship is down, is ready to be walked into the hangar.

An impressive sight. But always among the spectators are practical-minded men to raise practical questions.

A military reservation may carry a large force of men, since this is a part of their training, such spectators will argue, but it will be a heavy burden, perhaps an impossible one, for a private enterprise to carry on its payrolls a large force of men who may be kept busy only when a ship arrives or departs.

So this chapter should sketch the answer to this quite proper query and show how labor-saving machinery here as elsewhere, has been devised to conserve man-power and reduce costs.

Mechanical handling of large airships, while starting in England with the invention of the mooring mast a decade ago, was not taken up and developed actively until the U. S. Navy Department's work with the Shenandoah and the Los Angeles.

The chief reason why the mooring mast was devised elsewhere than in Germany, where the airship was born, is that Count Zeppelin, in selecting Friedrichshafen as the scene of his operations, chose perhaps the most nearly ideal location for this special purpose in all Europe. For Friedrichshafen has an equable climate and lies saucer-like in a natural basin surrounded by hills. So that it was possible to dock or launch an airship almost at will.

The problem of crews was simple too, for here as will be the case at the Goodyear-Zeppelin dock in Akron, workmen from the Zeppe-

(Photo by Rice—Montreal)

British ship R-100 moored to mast at Montreal, Canada, just after its transatlantic flight in 1930.

lin shops, specially trained, could be assembled on short notice to land a ship, would return to their places afterward, without necessitating extra men for this purpose and without interfering with the work in the shop.

The key part of the mooring mast is the cone at the top, mounted on a ball and socket arrangement so that it will swing in any direction, will move up and down. A cable, wound on a drum at the foot of the mast, leads up to the cone-shaped top, thrusts through that and outward and down to the ground. Then as the ship approaches the mast, heading to windward, with engines idling, it drops a line, as before. But this time the line is simply coupled to the line from the mast, the engine started up, the line wound up and the Zeppelin is slowly pulled forward until the nose is drawn into the mast cone, and great finger-like projections clamp down on it, holding the ship securely into place.

Instead of requiring 200 men to land a ship, this can be done at the mast by half a dozen.

Thus a ship coming into port when the wind is cross-hangar may moor to the mast and wait for better weather. A gangway is dropped permitting the passengers to go "ashore," ride down the small elevator within the mast's body, and go about their business. Refueling, regassing, ballasting and other services may also be had while the ship is moored out.

If the ship is in the dock and is to leave at a scheduled hour and the weather looks uncertain ahead, the commander will take advantage ahead of time of his first lull, to take the ship to the mast and wait there for the hour of departure. The sunrise and sunset lulls are frequently utilized in this way.

Indeed there is ample reason to expect that the mast, not the hangar or dock, will be the real terminal of the future, the shed being the dry dock and roundhouse of the air fleet, used for overhaul and repair.

However, the Navy Department was seeking, in conjunction with civilian engineers outside, further improvements in handling. In gusty inconstant weather, ballast had to be shifted frequently to put the ship in trim. The ship at the mast had always to be "flown." A wayward upward gust might kick the tail up 15 degrees before one could check it.

The first masts had been built to 180 feet and higher. Why not a shorter mast, with the ship almost resting on the ground? The wind could not come out of the ground itself. By lying low, it could lessen the effect of vertical currents. So a stub mast was built at Lakehurst and a carriage devised on which the after power car could rest, so that downward currents would not thrust it against the ground. This carriage was castored so that the ships could swing in any direction like a weather vane. The carriage ran on a circular track.

But another problem waited. Though a half dozen men could land a ship or set it loose for its journey, men would still be required if the ship was later to be taken into the dock. How would one solve that?

A mobile mast, telescopic, and mounted on three caterpillar trucks, pointed to the answer. As additional stability, the docking rails which course through the dock and emerge a ship's length beyond

Empire State Building, New York City, with Zeppelin mooring mast atop.

the doors, carry trolley cars, with ropes that can be quickly attached to the ship.

So the airship now may be drawn to the dock doors, don its harness of steel cables to check side gusts, and be marched in under cover.

The "iron horse" as the mobile mast at Lakehurst is called, points the way to mechanized handling of airships and indicates the practicability of landing and launching airships with no more man power than

Los Angeles moored to U. S. S. Patoka's mast.

1. Los Angeles moored to "iron horse" or mobile mast in use at Lakehurst, N. J. 2. Cradle used under the power car to permit free swing without damage to the ship when it is moored to a short or stub mast. (P. & A. Photo)

would be needed in ordinary service and maintenance work at a terminal with fewer men than needed to dock a large surface ocean vessel. The Graf Zeppelin used the mobile mast in landing and leaving Lakehurst in its American trip of 1930.

A similar mast was built at Akron in 1931 for the test-flights of the Navy ships, but with two of its caterpillars powered, so that towing was unnecessary.

There are at present six masts in the United States—navy masts at Lakehurst, Paris Island, Oahu, Hawaii, and Seattle, the army mast at Scott Field and the Ford mast at Detroit. A mast has been built on the navy tanker, the Patoka, and used successfully, indicating new possibilities of operating with the surface fleet.

An interesting innovation in mooring facilities was made in 1931 in the 200 foot mast, built complete with passenger elevator, winches and mooring cup, atop the Empire State Building in New York City, which became the tallest building in the world.

Likewise a portable mast has been worked out, and set up and successfully used at Coca Sola, the

U. S. S. Los Angeles, moored to mast at Lakehurst, N. J., U. S. Naval air station.

Canal Zone and at the Cleveland Air Races of 1929. The Graf Zeppelin landed to a temporary mast at Los Angeles on its world tour, using the navy mooring device from San Diego. It used a temporary mast at Seville and Pernambuco, Brazil, in its South American trip in 1930.

Impressive demonstration of the flexibility of Zeppelin mooring arrangements was made during the Navy maneuvers on the Carribean during February, 1931, when the Los Angeles operated with the fleet for almost a full month, landing to the Patoka on a temporary mast to refuel from time to time.

The Zeppelin Company built its first mast in 1929 at Berlin, Germany.

These various devices, initiated by the naval service, not only are valuable for commercial airships, but represent an important contribution to such a development in simplifying handling problems and conserving man-power. Indeed it may be that without such improvements, commercial operations might still be some way off instead of just around the corner.

New mobile mooring mast at Goodyear-Zeppelin dock, Akron.

CHAPTER XVII

Training Operations

SUCCESSFUL airship operation begins with fully trained officers and crew, both flying and ground personnel.

This training starts with the free balloon where variances in lifting forces due to changes in temperature, air pressure and altitude can be studied. As the free balloon is highly sensitive to wind directions and velocities and to changes in lift it forms an excellent training vehicle. It is also highly useful to the student in his observation of the weather and his interpretations of weather maps.

The motorized balloon or the non-rigid airship is the next step, for the student pilot now has forward speed and directional control, and can secure inexpensively in the small units the necessary experience in flying and landing an actual airship.

The last step in training is of course given on the large rigid airships. Along with the actual flying training goes an intensive class work study of the ship structure, the action of lifting gases under varied conditions, meteorology and navigation and operating methods.

1. For future commercial airships the Goodyear fleet is providing preliminary training in navigation, meteorology, radio, controls, motors and the handling of ships. This is the group of qualified pilots of the Goodyear fleet. 2. Jack A. Boettner, veteran airship and balloon pilot, under whose direction the Goodyear fleet pilots have been trained.

One of the world's smallest airships greets the world's largest ocean liner. The Puritan flying over the steamship Leviathan in New York harbor.

Such training is given carefully and thoroughly to successive classes of Naval officers at Lakehurst. Three of the most recent commanding officers of the Los Angeles, Lieutenant Commanders Rosendahl, Wiley and Clark have each had several years in flight training, and many others are being prepared for executive posts in the air navy.

The airship officer must know what to do not only under ordinary and normal conditions but under extraordinary and emergency conditions, and this knowledge must be built up through many hours of actual time aloft.

For future commercial airships, the Goodyear fleet is providing preliminary training in navigation, meteorology, radio, controls, engines, and the handling of ships, on the ground, in the air and in and out of docks. Some 60 men, many of them college and technically trained, some of them formerly in the army and navy services, completed their non-rigid training during 1930 at Akron, under J. A. Boettner, veteran airship and balloon pilot, and with the Volunteer at Los Angeles, under Lieutenant Commander Karl Lange, U. S. Naval Reserve, former airship officer at Lakehurst. This training will be invaluable to future commercial operations as the pilots of the small ships have had the experience of flight and handling operations.

Left: Elevator control stand or control room where fin surfaces or elevators of German Zeppelin ship L-59 were operated. Right: Control panel and elevator controls of one of Goodyear's airship fleet. Center: Airship Mayflower making a landing on the deck of the Bremen as it was anchored in quarantine. President P. W. Litchfield of the Goodyear-Zeppelin boarded the Mayflower and was flown to a New York City airport.

1. Navy Day celebration at Akron, Ohio, October 27, 1930, featured a helium toy balloon race participated in by high schools of the city. Some of the little spheres were located as far away as Massachusetts. 2. Admiral W. A. Moffett, Chief of the Bureau of Aeronautics for the Navy, and Miss Virginia Cooper who took part in a flag ceremony, presenting official colors for the Naval airship U. S. S. Akron. 3. At the Navy Day celebration at one of the schools. Left to right: O. C. Hatton, principal of East High school; M. M. Mell, representing the Akron Chamber of Commerce; Fred M. Harpham, vice president of the Goodyear Tire & Rubber Co., and a passenger on the Graf Zeppelin on one of its trips; Commander Garland Fulton, Chief of the Lighter-than-Air-Division of the Bureau of Aeronautics; Lt. T. G. W. Settle, in charge of Navy inspection at Akron; Admiral Moffett; T. W. Gosling, superintendent of Akron schools. 4. Silk flag purchased by penny donations of Akron school children and presented for them to the Navy by Miss Cooper. 5. The flag presentation which took place in the big airship dock. 6. Scene as viewed from catwalk. Airship framework visible at left.

CHAPTER XVIII

Commercial Air Liners

THE year 1930 opened not only with more activity in the field of lighter-than-air than has been seen since the World War, but with plans crystallizing in various parts of the world for airship lines connecting the continents—Europe and America, the two Americas, across the Pacific, lines connecting Orient and Occident.

Like the airplane, the airship was technically ready to take on the harness of transporting men and goods well ahead of the time it was called on to do so.

The Atlantic had been crossed both ways by the British R-34 as long as 11 years before. The Los Angeles had crossed it in 1924. The Graf Zeppelin had crossed the Atlantic three times before starting its world voyage in 1929.

Also, as in the case of the airplane, technical readiness was to wait for a single dramatic event which would challenge the consciousness of the public.

The airplane was no whit better the day after Lindbergh flew to Paris than it was the day before, but after that flight it became possible to finance airplane lines all over America. Dr. Eckener's world flight in the Graf Zeppelin appears to have performed a similar service for lighter-than-air.

Since the airship picture is changing—and rather rapidly—around the world, discussion of commercial operations may be obsolete before this edition of The Story of the Airship is well off the press. But one may survey some of the factors in the first projected all-American airship line, as an operation carefully thought through as to routes, cargo, and costs.

The British R-100, which made a successful round trip flight from England to Canada in 1930 was expected, after a period of government operation, to be operated by shipping interests over routes to Canada, Egypt, India. A hangar had been built in Karachi, India, supplementing those in England and mooring masts in Egypt and Canada, thus establishing terminal facilities for a British airship line from India to Canada—halfway round the world. With Sydney 12 days away by airship as against 28, with Montreal three days off, the British planned farsightedly to utilize this newest factor in transport and communication and to bring the Empire in closer touch with London.

In Germany the government encouraged the plans of Luftschiffbau-Zeppelin, the Hamburg-American Line and banking interests for transatlantic carrying. A new and larger hangar was being finished at Friedrichshafen and a new and greater Graf Zeppelin was under construction.

In Spain a subsidy had been

Artist's drawing of dining room in commercial air liner.

Artist's drawing of smoking room or lounge aboard commercial air liner.

made available for a company to set up a line between Seville and Buenos Aires. Japan built non-rigid ships, was considering the purchase of a rigid airship from Germany.

In America, the International Zeppelin Transport Co. has been chartered to study airship travel over the Atlantic, and the Pacific Zeppelin Transport Corporation, over the Pacific.

The ships would be similar in size, speed and general design to the Navy's "The Akron" except that accommodations for 40 to 100 passengers, sleeping and dining quarters, promenades, smoking room, shower baths and the other comforts of long distance travel would replace the simpler living necessities of a military ship.

The International Zeppelin Co. is headed by Col. E. A. Deeds, chairman; P. W. Litchfield, president; J. C. Hunsaker, vice president and general manager. The interests associated with it are Goodyear-Zeppelin, National City Co., G. M. P. Murphy & Co., Lehmann Bros., United Aircraft & Transport, Aluminum Company of America, and the Carbide & Carbon Chemicals Corp.

This corporation began during 1930 extensive investigations of the practicability of a transatlantic mail and passenger service by Zeppelin airships, including engineering studies of airships, terminals and operating practices, statistical studies of Atlantic weather and traffic, and finally ways and means to inaugurate scheduled flights.

Taking actual weather conditions as existing over the North Atlantic for a five-year period, the company's engineers made a series of theoretical flights, starting each Saturday night from Paris and Washington.

Knowing what weather they would have had to face had the flights been actual, with wind directions and velocities slowing up or speeding up their progress, they determined what routes would have been taken on each flight and what time each one would have required. More than 500 such flights were made.

These studies established the fact that the schedule of 2½ days for the eastward flight to Europe and of 3 to 3½ days for the return flight against prevailing winds was entirely practical. More exactly, that with a 58-hour schedule in the summer and 64-hour schedule in the winter for the eastward journey, and a 70-80-hour schedule returning, passenger airships would reach their destination on time or ahead of time 80 per cent of the journeys. They would never be as much as a day late and only twice in the five-year study were ships as much as 12 hours late.

The Great Circle route, skirting Newfoundland, which is the shortest route, would be used most of the year except in winter and even in that season there were many occasions when this route could be taken. On comparatively few occasions would it have been necessary to take the extreme southern route off Bermuda and the Azores.

Extensive terminal studies indicated that an American base could be established between Philadelphia and Richmond, located inland away from the force of the Atlantic gales and sheltered by the Blue Ridge to the West so that departures and arrivals could be made on schedule.

The plans of the company contemplated reciprocal use of terminals and traffic and service facilities with the German group, headed by Dr. Eckener, so as to avoid duplication of facilities, the German ships using the American hangars and masts, and vice versa.

Former Commander J. C. Hunsaker of the U. S. Navy, who is now vice president of the Goodyear-Zeppelin Corp. and president of the Pacific Zeppelin Co.

The European terminal would probably be located in the Rhine Valley about midway between Berlin and Paris and within a few hours' distance of London by airplane.

The Pacific project has special significance in any discussion of airships in that it includes among its directorate not merely financial interests in New York, the Pacific Coast, and Hawaii, but also the principal American steamship and airplane companies operating from the Pacific Coast.

The project was initially organized by three New York banking houses—Grayson M. P. Murphy & Co., Lehmann Bros. and the National City Co.—Col. Murphy and E. O. McDonnell of that company, Allen Lehmann and Roland Palmedo of Lehmann Bros., Col. E. A. Deeds and J. P. Ripley of National City being on the board of directors. On the board, too, are Edward P. Farley of the American-Hawaiian Steamship Line, R. Stanley Dollar of the Dollar Lines, W. P. Roth of the Matson Navigation Co., Harry Chandler of the Los Angeles Steamship Co.

Drawing showing promenade deck of airship to be used for passenger service.

Airplane transportation is represented by F. B. Rentschler, president of the United Aircraft and Transport Corp., G. B. Grosvener, president of The Aviation Corporation, C. M. Keys, president of Transcontinental Air Transport, J. A. Talbot, chairman of Western Air Express, Juan T. Hrippe, president of Pan-American Airways.

To these are added also Clarence H. Cooke of the Bank of Hawaii, John R. Galt of the Hawaiian Trust Co., and Walter Dillingham, representing the business interests of Honolulu, Herbert Fleischhacker of San Francisco, head of the Anglo-London-Paris Bank, Kenneth R. Kingsbury, president of the Standard Oil Co. of Calif., and Henry O'Melvany, attorney of Los Angeles. P. W. Litchfield, president of Goodyear Tire & Rubber Co. and of Goodyear-Zeppelin Corp., is chairman, and Commander J. C. Hunsaker, vice-president of Goodyear-Zeppelin Corp., is president of the Pacific Zeppelin Company.

The Pacific line would start with one ship, sailing between the Pacific Coast and Honolulu, continuing to Manila and the Orient later, as other ships were available and fuller operating experience had been acquired.

The first leg of this route, California to Hawaii, 2,200 miles, is perhaps the most favorable for airships of any of its length in the world. Following the path of the trade winds, the trip to Hawaii could be made in 36 hours and the return in 48, making weekly service to the islands a simple and practical operation.

It is 4,800 miles from Honolulu to Manila, 1,500 miles from there to Yokohama, 3,400 miles from Yokohama back to Honolulu. The trade winds would continue to follow the ships as far as Manila, and that trip could be made in three days. Head winds might be expected part of the time between Manila and Yokohama, but that flight should consume less than two days.

It may occur to the experienced traveler that hurricanes occur in certain months in the area around Manila, and this must be taken into account. Such a storm is of great intensity, but of local extent and follows a well defined track. With modern radio methods, its movements can be charted and its course predicted a day or more in advance.

A mooring mast would be erected at Guam and in case the radio reported bad weather at Manila, the ship could tie up to the mast and wait for it to blow over.

The return trip from Yokohama to California could be made nonstop, but the airships would probably stop at Honolulu for mail and passengers. The trip from Japan to America would then take from four to six days, depending on the season. One may contemplate then a trip from California to Manila via Hawaii in six days, returning via Japan in eight.

To provide legal status for the airship as a carrier of passengers, mail and express, the McNary-Parker bill, also called the Merchant Airship Act, was introduced in the 71st congress. In putting the measure in, Senator C. L. McNary, joint author with Congressman James L. Parker, stated:

"The purpose of the Merchant Airship Bill is to encourage construction in the United States by American capital of American airships for regular operations on our foreign trade routes by American operators. These airships are to be eligible for foreign mail contracts in accordance with the principles long established by Congress for the encouragement and protection of the American Merchant Marine. Airships eligible for the mail contracts must be capable of carrying not less than 10,000 pounds of mail and a suitable commercial load over distances in excess of 2,000 miles.

"As has been the case in aviation, much of the pioneering work done in the development of airships has been carried on by the Navy and War Departments. This development has reached a point where United States commercial enterprise, with reasonable encouragement and assistance from the government, is prepared to apply this new vehicle of transportation to foreign commerce. The development and operation of airships such as contemplated under this legislation would be of the utmost value to our national defense. The bill will make available, first, an American manufacturing industry with plants capable of meeting our national defense needs for airships; and, second, trained crews of American citizens capable of operating such airships."

CHAPTER XIX

Notable Airship Flights

LIGHTER-THAN-AIR set new records for long distance travel in 1930.

During the war, the L-59 made a 2,000-mile flight from Bulgaria across Egypt and the Sahara Desert, heading for German East Africa, with thirteen tons of ammunition and medical supplies for German troops who were besieged there, without other means of reenforcement than by airship.

Upon approaching its destination it was advised by wireless that the troops had capitulated, and the airship returned without landing or refueling, making a journey of 4,225 miles in 96 hours.

The British-built R-34 in 1919 flew from Pulham, England, to Mitchel Field, Long Island, a distance of 4,700 miles, in 108 hours, returning with more favorable winds in 75 hours.

The German built Dixmude, flown by the French, set a new distance and endurance record in 1923, flying from its base in Toulon across the Mediterranean to northern Africa and back, covering 4,500 miles in 119 hours.

The second aircraft to cross the Atlantic from east to west was the Los Angeles, in 1924, which made an even longer flight of 5,100 miles in 81 hours, flying from Friedrichshafen across Europe and the Atlantic to Lakehurst, N. J., where it was delivered to the U. S. Navy.

From coast to coast the Los Angeles was only 61 hours in the air, although it had to fly from the Azores to Newfoundland to circle a storm.

Another record was made by the Shenandoah in 1924 when it made a 9,317-mile flight from Lakehurst around the rim of the United States, stopping for fuel at Fort Worth, San Diego and Seattle, and back, being away from her hangar for 19 days and 19 hours, experiencing all varieties of weather and climate, much of it adverse.

Showing the potentialities of the airship in naval operations are two flights of the Los Angeles, from Lakehurst to Bermuda in 1925 in approximately 12 hours for each passage and a voyage to Porto Rico in 1925 in 31 hours. A nonstop flight of 2,250 miles to Panama in 37 hours and 20 minutes was made in 1928, the distance being 2,268 miles. A landing on the deck of the airplane carrier Saratoga in 1930 was another interesting example of the versatility of rigid ships.

The outstanding lighter-than-air achievement to date, however, was the around-the-world flight of the Graf Zeppelin in the summer of

1929. The Graf had already made a trip from Germany to Lakehurst in 1928 in 111 hours and 46 minutes, the return trip being made in 71 hours and 12 minutes.

During the summer of 1929, the Graf came to Lakehurst, and from there started on its return journey as the first leg of the world flight. It carried passengers, express and mail. The journey from Lakehurst to Lakehurst was completed in 21 days, seven hours and 33 minutes elapsed time, the actual flying time, exclusive of refueling stops at Friedrichshafen, Tokio and Los Angeles being but eleven days.

The Graf covered more than 21,700 miles on the trip, spanning two oceans and three continents. The 4,200 miles to Friedrichshafen was the fastest airship crossing of the Atlantic, consuming but 55 hours and 24 minutes or two days from coast to coast. The 6,880 miles from there across the Siberian steppes to Tokio took 101 hours and 50 minutes. The 5,800-mile flight across the Pacific to Los Angeles was made in 78 hours and 58 min- utes. The last leg across the Ame can continent was completed in hours and 59 minutes.

On its return to Germany, ho ever, the Graf beat its own roun the-world record. The flight fr Lakehurst to Friedrichshafen to 67 hours and 34 minutes, so th the total time from Friedrichshaf to Friedrichshafen was 20 da four hours and 18 minutes.

The year 1930 saw two mc transatlantic flights. The Gr Zeppelin flew from Friedrichshaf to Pernambuco, Brazil, with a st for mail and passengers at Sevil Spain, in 103 hours; made a bri visit to Rio de Janeiro with ground landing, returning to Pe nambuco for fuel; flew north Lakehurst in 69 hours, 12 minute returned home, again stopping f half an hour at Seville.

The British R-100 made its fi important flight in July, 1930, g ing from Cardington, England, a mooring mast at Montre Canada, in 79 hours, returni home in 57 hours, a distance 3,592 miles.

CHAPTER XX

Akron and Its Airport

CENTER for lighter-than-air activities in the United States is the distinction claimed by Akron, Ohio, sometimes referred to as the "Friedrichshafen of America."

At the eastern edge of this city of a quarter million, but within the corporation limits and three miles from the center of town, is the municipal airport of 900 acres, lying at an elevation of 1,040 feet above sea level in a natural basin flanked on two sides by low hills, unusually free from fog—a great level tract out of which rise the impressive arches of the Goodyear-Zeppelin Dock.

Thousands of visitors come out to the airport from all over t country every week. The Gr Zeppelin and the Los Angeles ha paid visits to the airport. Hu; Eckener has taken time to come Akron on each of his various tri to America. Here, too, come go ernment officials, members of Co gress, foreign visitors, scores delegations.

Akron did not win its place as air center over night. Airships a balloons have been a familiar sig at Akron for 15 years. The ci was an important training poi for lighter-than-air through t World War.

In addition to a municipal ai

port, Akron has a second flying field entirely devoted to lighter-than-air. This is at Wingfoot Lake, 12 miles southeast, a war-time aviation base, but now used by Goodyear's non-rigid fleet.

Akron, being a town set on the hills, straddling the Great Divide which separates the waters of the St. Lawrence from those of the Mississippi, it was not easy to find a level space large enough to build an airport. The site chosen was made level only through the moving of 1,800,000 cubic yards of earth and an expenditure by the city of more than $2,000,000, matching the Goodyear's expenditure for its dock. Although the airship dock dominates the skyline it occupies a tract of some 60 acres at one corner of the port to the southwest, in the line of the prevailing winds, the rest of the field being used for heavier-than-air operations.

At one part of the field, presently, a mooring mast will be erected; in another corner a $350,000 research laboratory is being constructed with funds made available by the Guggenheim Foundation and the city. The Guggenheim Research Laboratory, the only one in America to be devoted to lighter-than-air, will be administered by the University of Akron under the technical direction of California Institute of Technology.

Akron airport, reflected the vision and energy of the city

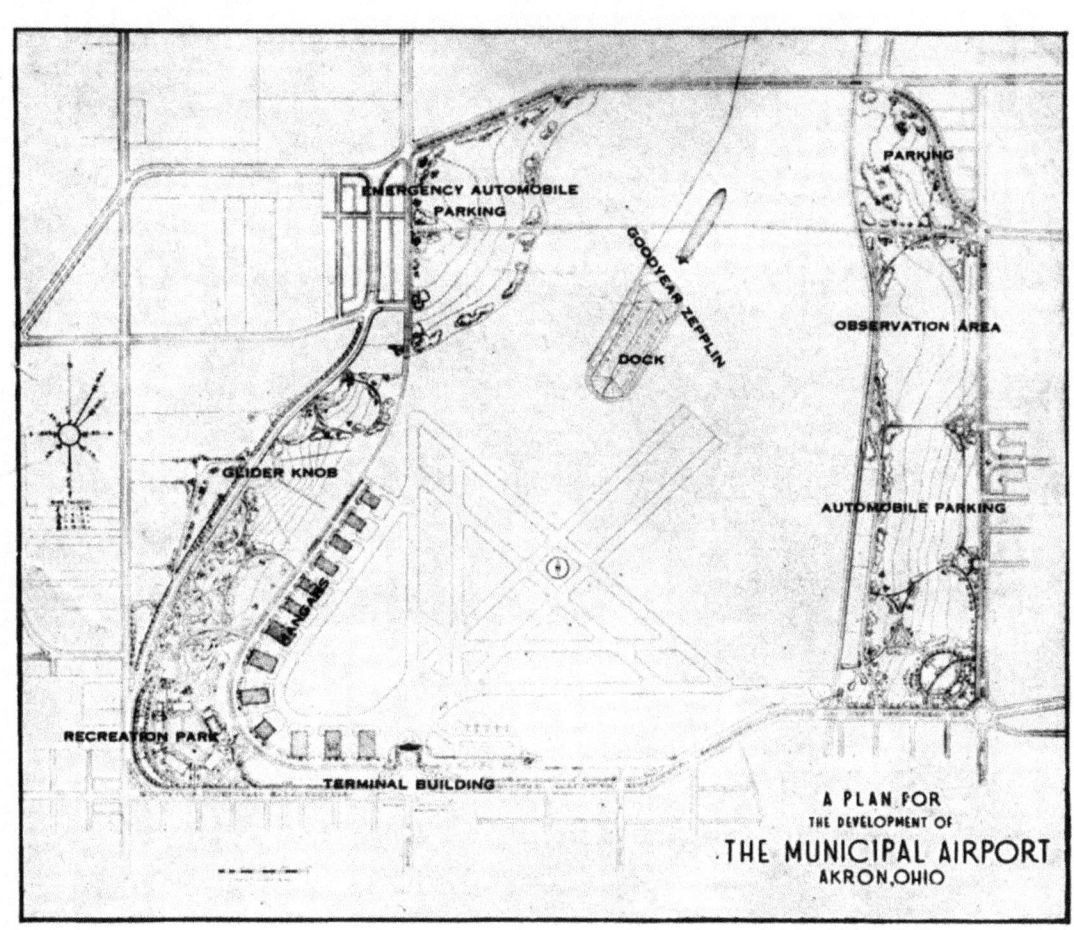

Drawing of the layout of Akron Municipal Airport. The buildings completed so far include: One heavier-than-air hangar, the municipal airport terminal building and the Goodyear-Zeppelin airship dock.

council, city and county officials and the Akron Chamber of Commerce who worked with far sighted citizens to bring it into existence.

* * *

The airship, older than the airplane, has been slower to find its place in transportation since the war. Political restriction in the case of Germany, the pioneer, the necessity for laborious and continued study both of construction and operation on the part of other nations, the necessity as well for large expenditures of courage and faith no less than of money and research, in so vast a project has forced airship development to proceed more slowly than in the case of other vehicles of transport.

Airplanes breed like rabbits, airships like elephants, Charles Gray, London editor, once said. But no one may visit the city of Akron without being impressed with the conviction that the airship industry in this country is being built on substantial foundations, that Akron with its concentration of technical and flying experience is doing its part to put America in a position to secure from the airship the advantages which that vehicle offers to civilization.

Graf Zeppelin being berthed in the Navy dock at Lakehurst, N. J., August, 1929, (P. & A. Photo).

After Word

David S. Ingalls, Assistant Secretary of Navy on aeronautics.
(Acme News Pictures.)

THE recent participation of the airship Los Angeles in Fleet war game maneuvers off Panama has provoked renewed discussion as to whether airships of this type are in fact useful to a modern Navy. As an observer aboard the Los Angeles for the better part of three days and nights, I was exceedingly gratified at the marked success attendant upon her use, although employed only in a scouting capacity and no defense of her at all was attempted. The results obtained from this single operation with this seven year old airship should be regarded as only a hint of what will be possible to accomplish with our two modern airships now under construction.

I consider the results obtained with lighter-than-air development to date have conclusively established that these craft are of material value in naval operations at sea and in defense of our coasts, and that the necessity of continued development and maintenance of lighter-than-air by the United States Navy has been proved.

Within the Navy, airship development has been regarded and handled as a giant experimental project. Frequently it has been criticised as expensive beyond a reasonable return for our investment. When other nations faltered and were on the verge of abandoning airship development, we alone had the courage to carry on. I believe we are approaching the time when the public will come to realize that this determination to go forward was based on foresightedness and not visionary dreams.

A public accustomed now to seeing airplane development go forward year by year in steady progress seems to have received the impression that airships are always battling against heavy odds. In the nature of things, airship development must be slower. These craft are larger, cost more to build, and require the concurrent creation of proper terminal facilities.

* * *

TO the commercial side of airships, the Navy's work must be of inestimable value. The change from surface transport to air travel has been very largely accomplished so far as land distances are concerned and the new influence on our daily life is beginning to be apparent. But the task of negotiating long non-stop distances over water carrying passengers and useful quantities of goods still baffles the airplane and flying boat. It is in this work that the airship seems likely to excel. Airships will prove to be the internationalists in our family of aircraft and by speeding up the correspondence of the business man, his contracts, and his money, will enable him to act more quickly and to go farther afield. In minimizing large ocean distances, large airships seem likely to prove themselves a mode of transportation that will be of tremendous significance to mankind. Nations will be drawn closer together, promoting increased co-operation and better understanding. It will be well for those interested in aeronautical development to pay more attention to airships and to make fair appraisal of the capabilities of these Leviathans of the air.

David S. Ingalls

Assistant Secretary of the Navy
for Aeronautics

Reprinted from National Aeronautic Magazine, April 1931

1. Friedrichshafen hangars at Luftshiffbau-Zeppelin Corp. at night. 2. Army airship docks at Ross Field near Los Angeles. 3. Airship dock for small ships built by Col. E. H. R. Green on his estate at Round Hill, Mass., and used by the Mayflower for two years. 4. Aerial view of Wingfoot Lake dock, Akron.

1. Airship dock of the U. S. Army at Scott Field, Belleville, Ill. 2. Inflation net and keel of RS ship in dock at Scott Field. 3. British hangar at Karachi, India. 4. Airship Shenandoah under construction in U. S. Navy airship dock at Lakehurst, N. J.

Appendix

A Page of Facts About the Goodyear-Zeppelin Airship Dock

The principal data and quantities of materials used are approximately as follows:

Length, center to center end doors, 1,175 feet.
Width, center to center hinges, 325 feet.
Height, center to center hinges, 197 feet, 6 inches.
Total floor to platform 211 feet.
Interior floor area 364,000 square feet.
Cubical content 55,000,000 cubic feet.
Perimeter of arch 562 feet.
Area of roof, 693,000 square feet.
Vertical sash 28,000 square feet.
Skylights 23,000 square feet.
Ventilators eight at 6 foot diameter.
Airplane doors 1,580 square feet.
Metal doors 2,612 square feet.
Inlet louvres 1,600 square feet.
Piling 1,300 required about 25 feet long.
Concrete foundations, etc., 8,000 cubic yards.
Concrete floors, 7,000 cubic yards.
Reinforcing steel 700 tons.
Structural steel in shell and shops, etc., 5,500 tons.
Structural steel in doors, 1,900 tons.

ENGINEERING PERSONNEL:

P. W. Litchfield, President, Goodyear-Zeppelin Corporation.
Dr. Karl Arnstein, Director of Engineering, Goodyear-Zeppelin Corporation.
W. C. State, Consulting Engineer, Goodyear-Zeppelin Corporation.
Wilbur Watson & Associates, Architects and Engineers.

SIZES OF PRINCIPAL AIRSHIP DOCKS

Dock	Dimensions
Goodyear-Zeppelin, Akron	1,175 x 200 x 325
Navy, Lakehurst, N. J.	780 x 170 x 258
Army, Scott Field, Belleville, Ill.	800 x 123 x 150
Army, Langley Field, Va.	450 x 125 x 125
Navy, Cape May, N. J.	708 x 109 x 106
Wingfoot Lake, Akron	400 x 95 x 100
Navy, Chatham, Mass.	250 x 66 x 100
Navy, Pensacola, Fla.	250 x 66 x 82
Army, Aberdeen, Md.	220 x 70 x 70
British, Cardington	812 x 156 x 181
British, Karachi, India	850 x 170 x 200
German, Friedrichshafen	775 x 158 x 181
German, Berlin (Staaken)	787.5 x 114.8 x 137.8
French, Orly	984 x 178 x 298
French, Toulon (Cuers)	770 x 150 x 197
Japanese, Tokio (Kasumiga-ura)	770 x 150 x 197
Miami, Fla., Municipal	250 x 120 x 70
Gadsden, Ala., Goodyear	200 x 86 x 70
Los Angeles, Goodyear	140 x 60 x 58
New Bedford, Mass.	140 x 60 x 58
St. Petersburg, Fla., Municipal	140 x 60 x 58
Holmes Airport, N. Y.	200 x 86 x 70

Some Important Facts About the Airship ZRS-4 or U. S. S. Akron

Nominal Gas Volume, Cu. Ft.	6,500,000
Length Overall, Ft.	785
Maximum Diameter, Ft.	132.9
Height Overall, Ft.	146.5
Gross Lift, Lbs.	403,000
Useful Lift, Lbs.	182,000
Number of Engines	8
Total Horsepower	4,480
Maximum Speed, M. P. H.	84
Range at 50 M. P. H. Cruising Speed Without Refueling, Miles	10,580

HULL

Built on triple-layer principle having (1) rigid metal framework to withstand major stresses, (2) gas cells within to retain lifting gas, and (3) a taut, fabric outer cover. Framework composed mainly of transverse rings connected by longitudinal girders. Most of rings are 36-sided polygons, with corners connected by longitudinal girders. Number of sides reduces to 24 near tail of ship. Network of diagonal wires forms bracing for outside panels. Ring girders of two types, main and intermediate. Main rings constructed in form of triangle, a new feature in airship construction, adding much strength. The main ring girders are spaced about 74 feet apart, gas cells being placed between them. There are 12 gas cells in the ZRS ships. Intermediate ring girders are of the single type and are spaced between the main girders, usually three to a compartment.

The longitudinal girders connect the ring girders, forming the fore and aft ridges discernible on the outside of the completed ship. Throughout most of the length of the ship extend three corridors or gangways, triangular in shape. One extends along the top center line of the ship, while the other two are placed symmetrically in the lower part, about 45 degrees from the vertical.

SHAPE

Modern design shows more curved profile, making ship appear slightly shorter and fatter than war types, which were shaped like lead pencil.

OVER-PRESSURE GAS VALVES

As lifting gas expands and contracts with changes in temperature, altitude and barometric pressure, valves are provided for immediate release of any surplus expansion. These are located in the gangway at the top, there being as many as four in the largest cells. They open automatically or may be opened mechanically from the control car.

EMPENNAGE

The control surfaces by which the ship is steered are located in pairs near the stern of the ship. Fixed sections give stability, while hinged after-sections or rudders give altitude and direction control.

CONTROL CAR AND QUARTERS

The control car is forward and contains latest devices for navigation. A radio cabin and commanding officers' quarters are directly over the car in the hull. A number of rooms for officers and crew are located near the middle of the ship along each side gangway. Each sleeping room has four comfortable berths. Messrooms and large galley are provided.

POWER PLANTS

Use of non-inflammable helium allows location of motors inside the ship's hull instead of being suspended in cars outside the hull, as is the case when hydrogen is used. There are four engines on each side of the ship. Rigid drive shafts, supported by outriggers, deliver power to the propellers outside the hull. Each propeller can be tilted on its axis through 90 degrees, by means of a special bevel gear, making it possible to use them in a vertical direction, instead of only fore and aft, the motors themselves being reversible. The feature of tilting propellers will be of great value in starting and landing maneuvers.

SAFETY

Among safety factors are the triple-layer hull; great structural strength; retention of gas in 12 separate cells; eight propulsion units; minimizing of fire risk by use of non-inflammable helium gas; accessibility of all parts of the ship while in flight, enabling repairs to be made, and action of the hull framework as a Faraday cage, protecting the ship against damage by lightning.

PASSENGER CARRYING

Structural design of navy ships may be easily adapted for commercial work, allowing accommodations to be built in for 100 passengers. Deck area of 12,000 square feet is provided, with staterooms of 70 square feet; 900 feet of corridors five feet in width; and ample promenades, lounges, dining rooms and smoking rooms will be in evidence. Lack of noise, odors and seasickness over oceans are three of the advantages of commercial airships. Another advantage is speed in long distance travel.

PRINCIPAL MOORING MASTS

United States—Lakehurst, N. J.	180 feet
Low Mast	60 feet
Scott Field	176.5 feet
Detroit (Ford)	216 feet
Hawaii	160 feet
Navy, Parris Island, S. C. (Low mast)	60 feet
Seattle, Wash.	160 feet
New York (Empire State Building)	200 feet

The Airship Tender Patoka also carries a mooring mast for airship operations with the fleet.

Great Britain—Pulham and Cardington, England; Montreal, Canada; Ismaelia, Egypt and Karachi, India, each 200 feet high.

Germany—Berlin (Staaken) 60 feet high.

Building the Dock

Contractors and principal suppliers in construction of Goodyear-Zeppelin Airship Dock:

MacArthur Concrete Pile Corporation, New York, concrete piling.
The Cable Company, Akron, grading.
The Clemmer-Noah Construction Co., Akron, concrete work and general.
The American Bridge Company, Pittsburgh, structural steel for main structures.
H. H. Robertson Company, Pittsburgh, roofing, windows, small doors, etc.
The Wellman Engineering Co., Cleveland, operating equipment for main doors.
The Kraus Plumbing & Heating Co., Akron, plumbing and sewering.
The Carle Electric Construction Co., Akron, electric wiring.
Otis Elevator Company, Cleveland, inclined elevators.
The Detroit Steel Products Co., Detroit, airplane doors.
The Burger Iron Company, Akron, structural steel for small buildings and details.
The Donley Bros. Co., Akron, concrete inserts.
The Forbs-Stanford Co., Akron, fire lines and hydrants.
Cleveland Crane and Engineering Co., Euclid, Ohio, cranes.
Morrison Railway Supply Co., Pittsburgh, railroad rails.

Building the Airship

Manufacturers who supplied substantial volume of materials or equipment for U. S. S. Akron:

Aero Supply Mfg. Corp., Corry, Pa. nickle and steel bolts.
Allison Engineering Co., Indianapolis, transmission gearing.
Aluminum Co. of America, Pittsburgh, duralumin.
American Brass Co., Waterbury, Conn., bronze and manganese.
American Cable Co., New York City, aircraft cable for control lines.
American Cellutex Corp., New York City, acetate celluloid windows for control car.
American Felt Co., Chicago, felt washers.
American Magirus Fire Appliance Co., Indianapolis, ladders.
American Rolling Mill Co., Middletown, armco iron.
American Steel and Wire Co., Worcester, Mass., mooring cables and wire network in ship.
Balsa Wood Co., New York, Balsa wood for flooring, catwalk, and partition.
Boston Insulated Wire and Cable Co., Boston, electric wiring.
Buffalo Forge Co., Buffalo, blower fans.
Buhl Stamping Co., Detroit, exhaust manifold.
Chase Brass and Copper Co., Waterbury, Conn., brass and copper.
Cleveland Pneumatic Tool Co., Cleveland, resiliency devices.
Cleveland Tool and Supply Co., Cleveland, miscellaneous supplies.
Crescent Panel Co., Louisville, Ky., plywood.
Dickerson Steel Co., Dayton, steel.
Eugene Dietzgen Co., Chicago, drafting supplies.
Dodd Co., Cleveland, drafting supplies.
DuPont Cellophane Co., Wilmington, Del., cellophane.
East Akron Hardware Co., Akron, mill supplies.
Eaton Axle and Spring Co., Cleveland, fuel tank fittings.
Eaton Spring Corp., Detroit, coil springs.
Eclipse Airbrush Co., Chicago, airbrush equipment for spraying outer cover.
Economy Scaffold Co., Chicago, scaffold around ship.
Electrical Maintenance Co., Youngstown, Ohio, electrical supplies.
Elgin National Watch Co., aircraft instrument division, Chicago—specially adjusted clocks for engine rooms.
B. K. Elliott Co., Cleveland, drafting supplies.
Euclid Crane and Hoist Co., Euclid, Ohio, cranes and hoists.
Everitt Co., Boston, small brass parts—bolts, nuts, cotter pins.
Fafnir Bearing Co., New Brittain, Conn., bearings in pulleys and control equipment.
Ferry Machine Co., Kent, Ohio, valves and machinery parts.
Fisher Scientific Co., Pittsburgh, instruments.
Forbes Varnish Co., Cleveland, Ohio, aluminum mixing varnish on frame work.
Fort Pitt Spring Co., Pittsburgh, coil springs.
Freitag Mfg. Co., Akron, dies.
Gears and forgings, Cleveland, forged gears.
General Electric Co., Schenectady, N. Y., electric instruments.
General Electric Supply Co., Akron, electric supplies.
General Fireproofing Co., Youngstown, aluminum furniture.

Graybar Electric Co., Chicago, electric supplies.
Great Lakes Aircraft Corp., Cleveland, dies and special channels.
Hagan Corp., Pittsburgh, blowers for heating system.
Halcomb Steel Co., Syracuse, tool steel.
Hall Rod Works, Highland Mills, N. Y., ramie cord for lacing outer cover on.
Hardware and Supply Co., Akron, mill supplies.
Harshaw Chemical Co., Cleveland, Ohio, anodic treatment acids.
Hartzell Propeller Co., Piqua, Ohio, propellers.
Haskelite Mfg. Corp., Chicago, plywood.
Herman Machine & Tool Co., Tallmadge, Ohio, automatic machine parts.
Herold Mfg. Co., Cleveland, acetate dope brushes.
Herman A. Holz, New York City, research instruments.
Imperial Brass Mfg. Co., Chicago, sanitary washroom equipment.
Independent Pneumatic Tool Co., Aurora, Ill., electric drills.
Kellogg Switchboard and Supply Co., Chicago, switchboard and telephones.
Kendall Refining Co., Bradford, Pa., oil for motor tests.
Walter Kidde and Co., New York City, fire extinguishing equipment.
Krout and Fite Mfg. Co., Philadelphia, binding tape.
Leeds and Northrup Co., Philadelphia, electric furnace control for heat treating equipment.
Linde Air Products Co., Cleveland, oxygen for welding.
Liquidometer Corp., Long Island City, N. Y., gauges.
Lyman Hawkins Lumber Co., scaffolding lumber.
Macwhyte Co., Kenosha, Wisc., tie rods.
Malin and Co., Cleveland, piano wire.
Manufacturers Rubber & Supply Co., Akron, alemite fittings.
Romec Pump Co., Elyria, Ohio, fuel pumps.
Maybach Motor Co., Friedrichshafen and New York, motors.
McKinney Tool and Mfg. Co., Cleveland, channel forming machinery.
Metallurgical Laboratories, Inc., Philadelphia, exhaust pipes.
Midland Steel Co., Cleveland, docking rails.
Midvale Co., Philadelphia, mooring and nose cone forging, chrome, nickel, molybdenum.
Morrison Railway Supply Co., Pittsburgh, rails for dock.
Motometer Co., Toledo, gauges.
National Lead Co., Cleveland, solder.
National Oxygen Co., Chicago, oxygen.
National Screw & Mfg. Co., Cleveland, screws and bolts.
National Sherardizing and Machine Co., Hartford, Conn., sherardizing.
National Steel Products Co., Dayton, fuel valves.
Oakite Products, Inc., New York, cleaning compound for dural.
Ohio Seamless Tube Co., Shelby, steel tubing.
M. O'Neil Co., Akron, miscellaneous supplies.
Ornamental Iron Works Co., Akron, steel scaffolding.
Paasche Airbrush Co., Chicago, airbrush equipment.
Paragon Revolute Co., Rochester, N. Y., blue print machinery.
Patent Scaffolding Co., Chicago, scaffolding.
W. M. Pattison Supply Co., Cleveland, mill supplies, fuel line fittings.
C. F. Pease and Co., Chicago, drafting supplies.
Penn Rivet Corp., Philadelphia, rivets.
Perry Austen Mfg. Co., New York, N. Y., acetate dope.
Pierce Butler and Pierce, Akron, mill supplies.
Pioneer Instrument Co., Brooklyn, N. Y., gauges.
Pittsburgh Plate Glass Co., glass for control car.
Piqua Electric and Mfg. Co., Piqua, ventilator fans.
Portage Iron and Wire Co., Akron, structural fixtures.
Fredrick Post Co., Chicago, drafting paper.
Quickwork Co., St. Mary's, Ohio, shop machinery.
Radium Dial Co., Ottowa, Ill., radium painting on instruments.
Reliance Mfg. Co., Massillon, Ohio, stainless steel lock washers.
Republic Steel Corp., Alloy Division, Massillon, Ohio, stainless steel for fuel line fittings, exhaust manifolds.
Republic Structural Iron Works, Inc., Cleveland, structural iron manifolds.
Revere Copper and Brass, Inc., Boston, brass and copper.
John A. Roeblings Sons, Trenton, N. J., aircraft cable.
Rome-Turney Radiator Co., Rome, N. Y., radiators (motors).
J. T. Ryerson and Son, Inc., shop machinery.
SKF Industries, New York, bearings.
Shakeproof Lockwasher Co., Chicago, lock washers.
Sherwin-Williams Co., Cleveland, aluminum mixing varnish for ship structure.
Silica-Gel Corp., Baltimore, dehydration equipment for drying air before dope is sprayed on.
Simplex Wire and Cable Co., Boston, special electric wiring.
A. O. Smith Corp., Milwaukee, helium storage tanks.

Spaulding Fibre Co., N. Tonawanda, N. Y., hard fibre.
W. K. Stamets Co., Pittsburgh, shop machinery.
Stanley Works, New Britain, Conn., duralumin hardware.
State Foundry & Machine Co., Akron, cast iron castings.
Steel Products Engineering Corp., Springfield, Ohio, propeller hubs.
Steel and Tubes, Inc., Cleveland, steel tubing.
Edwin B. Stimpson Co., Brooklyn, grommets, brass and duralumin.
Summerill Tubing Co., Bridgeport, Pa., steel tubing for propeller outriggers.
Super Steels, Inc., Cleveland, alloy steel.
Tappan Stove Co., Mansfield, Ohio, cooking stove.
Taylor Instrument Co., Rochester, N. Y., thermometers.
Texas Co., Chicago, gas for motor tests.
W. Harris Thurston, New York City, outer cover, gas cell cloth.
John S. Tilley Ladders Co., Inc., Watertown, N. Y., ladders and horses.
Tide Water Oil Co., New York., Veedol oil for motor tests.
Toledo Scale Co., Toledo, scales.
Townsend Co., New Brighton, Pa., iron rivets.
W. S. Tyler Co., Cleveland, wire mesh.
U. S. Automatic Co., Amherst, Ohio, automatic machine parts.
U. S. Radium Co., New York., radium, painting instruments.
U. S. Steel Wire Spring Co., Cleveland, coil springs.
J. C. Ulmer Co., Cleveland, dies.
Ultra Fuzon Distributing Co., New York, fireproof paint for engine rooms.
United Screw and Bolt Co., Cleveland, aircraft washers.
Universal Drafting Machine Co., Cleveland, drafting machines.
Universal Motor Co., Oshkosh, motor generator units.
Upson-Walton Co., Cleveland, ropes, tackle blocks.
Waltham Screw Co., Waltham, Mass., small instrument parts.
Edgar T. Ward's Sons Co., Pittsburgh, steel tubing and sheets.
Weber Brass Co., Cleveland, spinnings.
Westinghouse Electric & Mfg. Co., East Pittsburgh, radio electric motors and electrical equipment.
Weston Electric Instrument Co., Newark, N. J., electric instruments.
Whitney Metal Tool Works, Rockford, Ind., rivet squeezers.
Whitney Mfg. Co., Hartford, Conn., chains and sprockets for steering machinery.
Willard Storage Battery Co., Cleveland, storage batteries.
Williams and Co., Pittsburgh, International Metal Corp., monel metal.
Willis Co., (General Electric), rivet cooling equipment.
Wolverine Tube Co., Detroit, brass and copper tubing.
George Worthington and Co., Cleveland, mill supplies.
Yoho and Hooker, Youngstown, aircraft spruce.

Records Made in Goodyear-Constructed Free Balloons To January 1, 1930

The World's Altitude Record for balloons was made in a Goodyear bag by Captain H. C. Gray, A. C., U. S. A., 42,470 feet, using an 80,000 special spherical, on November 4, 1927.

Distance—W. T. Van Orman-C. K. Wollam, 1,080 miles, San Antonio, Texas, to Rochester, Minn., using an 80,000 spherical. 1924 National Balloon Race, San Antonio, Tex., April 23, 1924.

Duration—W. T. Van Orman-W. W. Morton, 51 hours, 31 minutes, using an 80,000 spherical. 1927 International Balloon Race for second Gordon Bennett trophy, Detroit, Mich., September 10, 1927.

History of Akron Participation In Ballooning

NATIONAL BALLOON RACES
For the P. W. Litchfield Trophy

	STARTING POINT	FINISH
R. H. UPSON, Pilot R. A. D. PRESTON, Aide	July 4, 1913— Kansas City, Mo.*	W. Branch, Mich.—20 hrs.
R. A. D. PRESTON, Pilot M. D. TREMELIN, Aide	July 11, 1914— St. Louis, Mo.*	Constance, Ky.—24¾ hrs.
RALPH H. UPSON, Pilot W. T. VAN ORMAN, Aide	Oct. 1, 1919— St. Louis, Mo.*	Montreal, Que.—27 hrs.
RALPH H. UPSON, Pilot W. T. VAN ORMAN, Aide	Sept. 25, 1920— Birmingham, Ala.†	Lorain, O.—38 hrs.
W. T. VAN ORMAN, Pilot †††W. P. SEIBERLING, Aide	May 21, 1921— Birmingham, Ala.†	Nashville, Tenn.—20 hrs.
W. T. VAN ORMAN, Pilot W. W. MORTON, Aide	May 30, 1922— Milwaukee, Wis.	Kansas City—28 hrs.
W. T. VAN ORMAN, Pilot HERBERT THADEN, Aide	July 4, 1923— Indianapolis, Ind.	Ft. Wayne—4 hrs.
J. A. BOETTNER, Pilot J. M. YOLTON, Aide	July 4, 1923— Indianapolis, Ind.	Sandusky, O.—14 hrs.
W. T. VAN ORMAN, Pilot C. K. WOLLAM, Aide	April 23, 1924— San Antonio, Tex.*	Rochester, Minn.—44 hrs.
W. T. VAN ORMAN, Pilot C. K. WOLLAM, Aide	May 1, 1925— St. Joseph, Mo.*	Birmingham—43 hrs.
W. T. VAN ORMAN, Pilot W. W. MORTON, Aide	April 29, 1926— Little Rock, Ark.*	Norfolk, Va.—43 hrs.
J. A. BOETTNER, Pilot H. W. MAXSON, Aide	April 29, 1926— Little Rock, Ark.†	Welch, Va.—36 hrs.
W. T. VAN ORMAN, Pilot W. W. MORTON, Aide	May 30, 1927— Akron, Ohio*	Bar Harbor, Me.—26 hrs.
J. A. BOETTNER, Pilot J. F. COOPER, Aide	May 30, 1927— Akron, Ohio	Montreal—25 hrs.
C. K. WOLLAM, Pilot HOWARD WOLFE, Aide	May 30, 1927— Akron, Ohio	Saranac Lake—21 hrs.
W. T. VAN ORMAN, Pilot W. W. MORTON, Aide	May 30, 1928— Pittsburgh, Pa.	Greensburg, Pa.—2 hrs.
C. A. PALMER, Pilot JOS. MELL, Aide	May 30, 1928— Pittsburgh, Pa.	Annapolis, Md.—18 hrs.
C. K. WOLLAM, Pilot J. F. COOPER, Aide	May 30, 1928— Pittsburgh, Pa.	Greensburg, Pa.—2 hrs.
W. T. VAN ORMAN, Pilot A. L. MacCRACKEN, Aide	May 14, 1929— Pittsburgh, Pa.‡	Plattsburg, N. Y.—21 hrs.
R. J. BLAIR, Pilot FRANK TROTTER, Aide	July 4, 1930— Houston, Tex.*	Greensburg, Ky.—48 hrs.

*—Won first place.
‡—Won second place.
†—Won third place.
†††—Won by R. H. Upson.

INTERNATIONAL BALLOON RACES
For the James Gordon Bennett Cup

	STARTING POINT	FINISH
RALPH H. UPSON, Pilot R. A. D. PRESTON, Aide	Oct. 12, 1913— Paris, France*	Bridlington, Eng.—43 hrs.
RALPH H. UPSON, Pilot W. T. VAN ORMAN, Aide	Oct. 24, 1920— Birmingham, Ala.†	Windsor, Can.—44 hrs.
W. T. VAN ORMAN, Pilot W. P. SEIBERLING, Aide	Sept. 18, 1921— Brussels, Belgium	Exeter, Eng.—22 hrs.
W. T. VAN ORMAN, Pilot C. K. WOLLAM, Aide	June 15, 1924— Brussels, Belgium	Amsterdam, Hol.—37 hrs.
W. T. VAN ORMAN, Pilot C. K. WOLLAM, Aide	June 7, 1925— Brussels, Belgium	S. S. Vaterland, 60 miles off shore of Brest—30 hrs.
W. T. VAN ORMAN, Pilot W. W. MORTON, Aide	May 30, 1926— Antwerp, Belgium*	Solverborg, Swd.—17 hrs.
J. A. BOETTNER, Pilot H. W. MAXSON, Aide	May 30, 1926— Antwerp, Belgium	Amsterdam—3 hrs.
W. T. VAN ORMAN, Pilot W. W. MORTON, Aide	July 4, 1927— Detroit, Mich.†	Adrian, Georga—51 hrs., 31 minutes.
C. A. PALMER, Pilot FRANK McKEE, Aide	Sept. 6, 1928— Detroit, Mich.	Fairmount, W. Va.—22 hrs.
W. T. VAN ORMAN, Pilot A. L. MacCRACKEN, Aide	Sept. 28, 1929— St. Louis, Mo.*	Troy, Ohio—24 hrs.
W. T. VAN ORMAN, Pilot A. L. MacCRACKEN, Aide	Aug. 30, 1930— Cleveland*	Boston—27 hrs., 56 min.

*—Won first place.
†—Won third place.

WINNERS OF THE JAMES GORDON BENNETT BALLOON RACES

Year	Starting Point	Winner	Country
1906	Paris, France	F. P. LAHM	United States
1907	St. Louis, Mo.	O. ERBSLOH	Germany
1908	Berlin, Germany	COL. SCHAECK	Switzerland
1909	Zurich, Switzerland	E. MIX	United States
1910	St. Louis, Mo.	A. R. HAWLEY	United States
1911	Kansas City, Mo.	O. GERICKE	Germany
1912	Stuttgart, Germany	A. BIENAIME	France
1913	Paris, France	RALPH UPSON	United States
1920	Birmingham, Ala.	LT. DeMUYTER	Belgium
1921	Brussels, Belgium	CAPT. ARMBRUSTER	Switzerland
1922	Geneva, Switzerland	LT. DeMUYTER	Belgium
1923	Brussels, Belgium	LT. DeMUYTER	Belgium
1924	Brussels, Belgium	LT. DeMUYTER	Belgium
1925	Brussels, Belgium	VEENSTRA	Belgium
1926	Antwerp, Belgium	W. T. VAN ORMAN	United States
1927	Detroit, Mich.	E. J. HILL	United States
1928	Detroit, Mich.	W. E. KEPNER	United States
1929	St. Louis, Mo.	W. T. VAN ORMAN	United States
1930	Cleveland, Ohio	W. T. VAN ORMAN	United States

International Record—1,298 miles—Paris-Moscow—1912—Bienaime.
Clifford Harmon—48 hrs., 23 min.—St. Louis—1909.
Hawley Post 1910—1,172 miles—St. Louis-Lake St. Johns, Quebec.
Van Orman—San Antonio-Port Chester—44 hrs., 10 min.—1924.

Facts About Goodyear Fleet

Name of Ship	Christening Date	Length in Feet	Diameter in Feet	Gas Capacity Cubic Feet	Fuel Capacity Gallons	Motors and Horse-power	Speed Miles Per Hour	Cruising Range Miles	Hours Flown to May 1, 1931	Number of Flights to May 1, 1931	Passenger Capacity	Passengers Carried to May 1, 1931	Miles Flown to May 1, 1931
Pilgrim	July 25, 1925	110	32	55,000	40	One Lawrance 60 H.P.	38	440	2,222	3,169	2	3,097	73,260
Puritan	Aug. 6, 1928	134	39	96,000	100	Two Warner Scarab 110 H.P.	60	400	2,550	3,807	4	6,797	111,244
Volunteer	May 4, 1929	134	39	96,000	100	Two Siemens-Halske 70 H.P.	60	462	1,872	2,261	4	4,594	80,061
Mayflower	May 21, 1929	128	36	86,000	100	Two Siemens-Halske 80 H.P.	55	462	2,177	2,966	4	5,342	92,198
Vigilant	June 28, 1929	128	36	86,000	100	Two Siemens-Halske 80 H.P.	55	462	2,559	3,649	4	9,316	110,037
Defender	Aug. 30, 1929	184	43	178,000	330	Two Wright J-6 165 H.P.	62	1175	2,596	2,870	8	14,249	129,800
									13,976	18,722		43,395	596,600

Bibliography

"The Zeppelins," by Ernst Lehmann and Harold Mingoes—J. H. Sears & Co.

"Zeppelin, the Story of a Great Achievement," by Harry Vissering, Chicago, 1922.

"Taschenbuch der Luftflotten," by Rasch and Hormel; J. F. Lehmann publishers, Munich, Germany, 1914.

"British Airships," by G. Whale; John Lane, publishers, London, 1919.

"Commercial Airships," (including the flight of the R-34), by H. B. Pratt.

"Aerial Navigation," by Albert F. Zahm—Appleton.

"Die Amerikafahrt des Graf Zeppelin," by Brandt.

"Aircraft Yearbook," issued annually by Aeronautic Chamber of Commerce.

"Log of the R-34," by Major G. H. Scott.

"Building the World's Largest Airship," by Karl Arnstein; published by Goodyear-Zeppelin Corporation.

"Building the World's Largest Airship Factory and Dock," by Wilbur Watson; published by Goodyear-Zeppelin Corporation.

Various scientific papers by Commander Garland Fulton, U. S. N. (C. C.); by

Commander J. C. Hunsaker, U. S. N. (C. C.); by Dr. Karl Arnstein; by Ernst Lehmann.

"FREE AND CAPTIVE BALLOONS," by Ralph H. Upson, Ronald Press.

"AIRSHIP DESIGN," by Charles P. Burgess, Ronald Press.

"FUNDAMENTALS OF FLUID DYNAMICS FOR AIRCRAFT DESIGN," by Max M. Munk, Ronald Press.

"THE CONQUEST OF THE AIR," by John Alexander.

"AEROPLANES AND AIRSHIPS," by William E. Dommett.

"D'ORCY'S AIRSHIP MANUAL," by Ladislas D'Orcy.

"COMMERCIAL AIR TRANSPORT," by I. A. E. Edwards.

"DIRIGIBLE BALLOONS," by C. B. Hayward.

"AIRSHIPS, PAST AND PRESENT," by Alfred Hildebrandt.

"THE RIGID AIRSHIP," by Ernest H. Lewitt.

"AERIAL NAVIGATION," by Charles B. Mansfield.

"MY AIRSHIPS," by Santos Dumont.

"SCIENCE OF FLIGHT," by P. J. H. Sumner.

"AIRPLANES, AIRSHIPS, AIRCRAFT ENGINES," by Albert Tucker.

"AEROSTATICS," by Edward P. Warner.

"MILITARY OBSERVATION BALLOONS," by Emil J. Widmer.

"LUFTSCHIFF UND LUFTSCHIFFAHRT," Marinebaurat Engberding—Voi Verlag, Berlin.

"IM LUFTSCHIFF UBER HAMBURG," (also over Baden, and over Frankfort), by E. Gruettel and Dr. Karl Endriess, published by Luftschiffbau Zeppelin, Friedrichshafen.

"GRAF FERDINAND VON ZEPPELIN," Joseph Mayer. Verlags und Druekerei, Stuttgart.

"MIT GRAF ZEPPELIN NACH SUD—UND NORD AMERIKA," J. Breit haupt, Verlag von Moritz Schauenberg, Lahr (Baden).

"ZEPPELIN—DER MENSCH, HER KAEMPFER, DER SIEGER," Verlag von Robert Lutz, Stuttgart.

"ZEPPELIN—DENKMAL FUR DAS DEUTSCHES VOLK," Hans Hildebrandt—Germania Verlag, Stuttgart.

Airship Motion Pictures For Showing Sent Free

Several interesting motion picture films in 16mm and 35mm sizes, showing building of the U. S. S. Akron and the dock, the Goodyear fleet of non-rigid ships, the Graf Zeppelin's trip around the world and various subjects in aeronautics, and other films of an educational nature are supplied free for showing. Film catalogue sent on request. Address Motion Picture Division, Goodyear Tire & Rubber Company, Akron, O.

Aircraft At War DVD Series

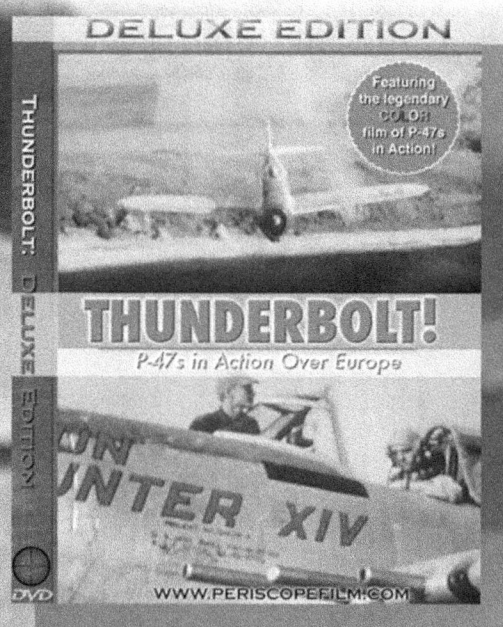
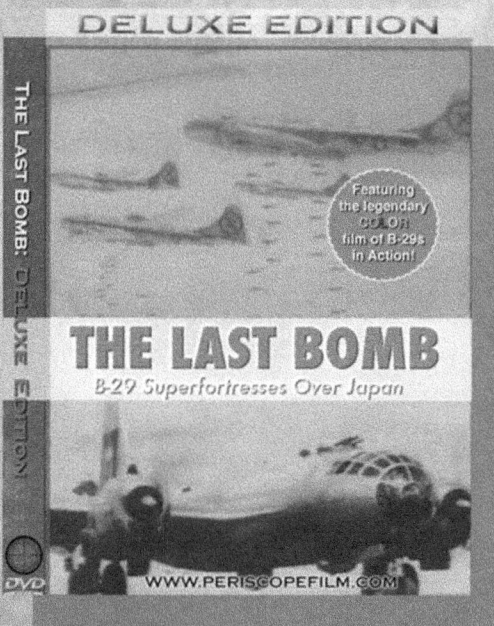

Now Available!

HUGHES FLYING BOAT MANUAL

SPRUCE GOOSE

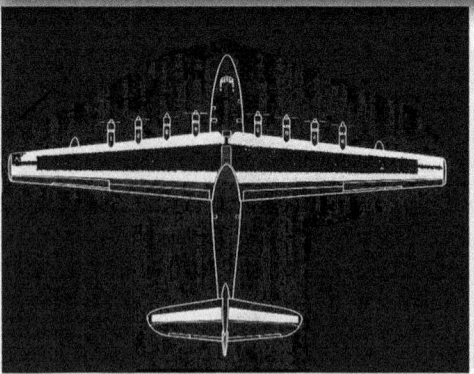

RESTRICTED

Originally Published by the War Department
Reprinted by Periscope Film LLC

NOW AVAILABLE!

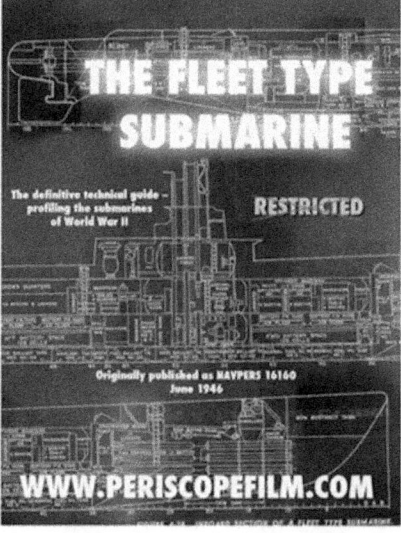
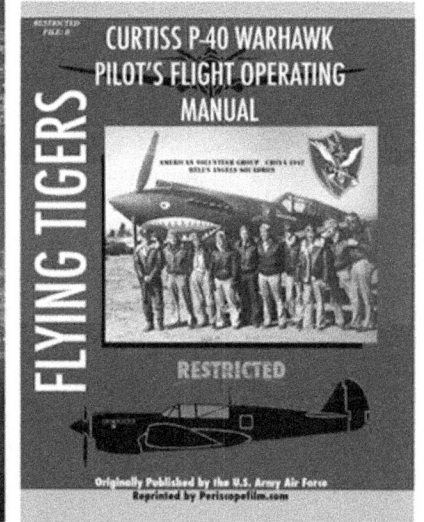

ALSO NOW AVAILABLE
FROM PERISCOPEFILM.COM

©2008-2010 Periscope Film LLC
All Rights reserved
ISBN # 978-1-935700-04-3
www.PeriscopeFilm.com

www.ingramcontent.com/pod-product-compliance
Lightning Source LLC
LaVergne TN
LVHW061346060426
835512LV00012B/2582